ENGLISH G

| G9 |

W0377243

access 5

WORKBOOK MIT INTERAKTIVEN ÜBUNGEN

Cornelsen

Vokabeltrainer-App

Verfügbar für: iOS, Android und Windows Phone

scook

AUDIOS online

Deine **interaktiven Übungen, Audios** und **Erklärfilme** findest du auf scook.de. Dort gibst du den unten stehenden Zugangscode in die Box ein.

nidaxu

Dein Zugangscode auf www.scook.de | gctr-tj-b33g

Cornelsen

Australia
country and continent

1 Welcome to Australia!
→ SB (pp. 12–13) • Wordbanks 1–2

Look carefully at the two pictures of Australia. What do they tell you about the country and about the life there? Which picture do you prefer, and why? Write down your ideas.

1

2

Picture 1

2 REVISION In a shop in Sydney (Simple present and present progressive) ➜ SB (p. 16) • GAP 1.3 (p. 64)

Put the verbs in brackets into the correct form: simple present or present progressive.

Assistant: Hi. *Are you looking* (you look) for anything special?

Student: Oh, hello. I ________________ (try) to find an Australian souvenir for my mum. She ____________ (live) in Germany.

Assistant: Wow, you're really far from home. ________________ (you learn) English here?

Student: Yes. I ________________ (do) a high school programme.

Assistant: That's great. I guess your English ______________________ (get) better every day. People here ____________________ (not learn) German at school very often. We ________________ (learn) Japanese and Mandarin as well as European languages.

Student: I also ________ (go) to a beginners' Japanese class three times a week after school. They ________ (give) us a lot of homework. So I __________________________ (really enjoy) my free day today.

Assistant: Oh, sorry, my boss ____________ (call) me. I'll be back in a second to show you some nice souvenirs.

3 REVISION Leon's first days at school (Simple past or past progressive) ➜ SB (p. 16) • GAP 2.1, 2.3 (p. 64)

Complete the sentences with the correct forms of the verbs in brackets: simple past or past progressive.

The night before his first day at the new school Leon *was feeling* (feel) really nervous because he ____________ (not know) what to expect. When he and Nick ____________ (arrive) the next morning, a lot of students ________________ (stand) outside the hall. Nick ________ (tell) Leon that everyone ____________ (wait) for assembly[1] and ____________ (show) him where to stand. After assembly, all the Australian students ________ (go) to their classrooms. While they ________________ (have) their first lessons, a coordinator ____________ (inform) Leon about the rules and routines at the school. Later Leon ____________ (join) his class and ______________ (introduce) himself to his classmates. Even though they all ____________ (give) him a warm welcome, he ____________ (remain) a bit shy. A few days later, when he ________________ (sit) in the playground by himself, he ____________ (notice) that a group of boys from his class ______________ (watch) him. Then they ________ (sit) down next to him and ____________ (ask) him a lot of questions about school life in Germany. While Leon ________________ (talk) to them, he suddenly ____________ (not feel) shy anymore. During his year in Sydney, he ________________ (become) good friends with the other students.

[1] assembly [əˈsembli] *Schülerversammlung*

4 WORDS Australia puzzle ➜ SB (p. 17)

Write the words in the puzzle. What's the word in the blue boxes?

1 the areas of Australia that are far away from cities
2 the Australian word for "friend"
3 connected with native Australians
4 connected with a town or city
5 the opposite of dry
6 difficult to reach

➜ _ _ _ _ _ _

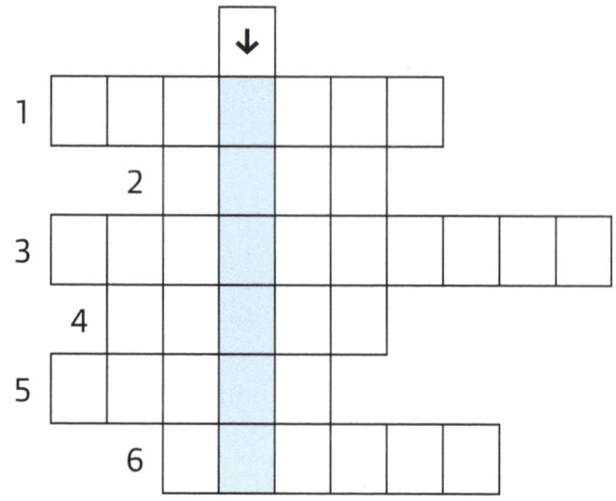

5 Australian sounds (Pronunciation of Australian English) ➜ SB (p. 17)

a) ○ 01 Listen and write the sentences.

1 ______________________ 3 ______________________

2 ______________________ 4 ______________________

b) 02 Listen to the statements. Are the people speaking British or Australian English? Write BE or AusE.

1 *BE, AusE* 3 ________ 5 ________ 7 ________

2 ________ 4 ________ 6 ________ 8 ________

6 REVISION About The Rocks (Relative clauses: *who* or *which*) ➜ SB (p. 18) • GAP 15.1 (p. 72)

a) ○ Circle the correct relative pronoun.

1 If you go to Sydney, you should visit The Rocks, a beautiful historical quarter who / which is very lively.
2 The first inhabitants to live there were the Gadigals, Aboriginals who / which called the area Tallawoladah.
3 Most people who / which came from Britain in the 18th century and settled in The Rocks were convicts.
4 The homes who / which these first settlers built for themselves were traditional English houses.

b) Fill in who or which.

1 The Rocks has more than 100 historical places ____________ give you an idea of life in colonial Australia.
2 Visitors ____________ want to know more about the history of The Rocks should take a guided tour.
3 In some parts of the quarter you can find nice markets and shops ____________ are popular with tourists.
4 Clothes, jewellery and art are just some of the things ____________ you can buy there.

7 Fun at Manly Beach (Participle clauses instead of relative clauses) ➜ *SB (p. 18)* • *GAP 16.2 (p. 73)*

a) Use a participle clause to make one sentence out of two.

1 Near the water there is a group of small children. They are having their first surfing lesson.

____

2 Look at the woman in the grey and red wetsuit.[1] She's riding a huge wave.

____

3 A girl is filming her boyfriend. He is trying to stand up on his surfboard.

____

4 Behind the young man you can see an excellent surfer. He's jumping and turning around easily.

____

b) ● Order the words and write the sentences in your exercise book.

1 a · watching · lifeguard[2] · there's · kitesurfers · the
2 playing · are · there · teenagers · beach volleyball · some
3 under · woman · reading · book · a · tree · a · is · a · sitting
4 the · there · near · good · are · food · beach · cafés · serving

8 What did they see, smell, hear? (Participle clauses after verbs of perception) ➜ *SB (p. 19)* • *GAP 16.3 (p. 74)*

Look at the pictures and use the phrases to complete the sentences below. Use participle clauses.

1 Leon noticed *Nick's dog eating a muffin.*

2 The tourists watched ______________________________

3 Cary saw ______________________________

4 The tourists saw ______________________________

5 Elvira smelt ______________________________

6 Tom listened to ______________________________

[1]wetsuit ['wetsu:t] *Taucheranzug* [2]lifeguard ['laɪfgɑ:d] *Rettungsschwimmer, -schwimmerin*

9 Discover Manly ➔ SB (p. 19) • SMC 21 (p. 83)

a) 03 You go on a tour of Manly. Listen to the guide and take notes about what you can see there.

b) After your tour you want to tell a German friend about what you saw and did in Manly. Write an email in German to your friend back home. Write it in your exercise book.

10 STUDY SKILLS Argumentative writing ➔ SB (p. 21) • SMC 8 (p. 78)

a) ○ Tick the correct answers.

1 In an argumentative text you …
- present only your personal arguments. ○
- present only arguments that you disagree with. ○
- present arguments for and against a position. ○

2 You form your opinion …
- before you start collecting arguments. ○
- after you have collected arguments. ○
- after you have written the text. ○

3 You structure your text …
- before you collect ideas. ○
- before you start writing. ○
- while you are writing. ○

4 You state and explain your opinion …
- in the introduction. ○
- in the main body. ○
- in the conclusion. ○

b) Find arguments for and against this statement: "Australians don't need to learn foreign languages."

For	Against
– English is a world language. – …	– Not everyone in the world speaks English. – …

c) Now write an argumentative text on this topic in your exercise book. Follow steps 1 to 5 on p. 21 of your student's book.

11 WORDS A year in Far North Queensland ➔ *SB (pp. 22–23)*

Complete 16-year-old Katharina's report about her experience as an exchange student in Far North Queensland. Use the words from the box.

bumped · business districts · coral reefs · crococile · easy-going · exotic · *flight* · humid · insects · poisonous · pythons · remote · rural · snorkelling · stunning · trendy · urban

I had heard a lot about FNQ, but nothing could really prepare me for that moment when my *flight* ______ landed and I went outside into the ______ air. Living in Cape Trib, I mainly experienced ______ – not ______ – Australia. There weren't many ______ cafés or ______ with skyscrapers there – just ______ regions with a lot of space, ______ landscapes and amazing marine ecosystems[1], like ______ ______. The ______ and sometimes scary wildlife soon became an everyday sight for me: ______ spiders, long ______ and biting ______ everywhere. One day I even saw a ______ while I was ______ at the beach – luckily it didn't see me! The best thing about the year was all the Aussies I met. I ______ into the same people all the time, because we lived in a small town. With such ______ mates, how could I ever be homesick?

12 Animals everywhere (Participle clauses) ➔ *SB (p. 24)* • *GAP 17.1 (p. 74)*

Rewrite the sentences, using a participle clause.

1 After dinner we sat outside and listened to the insects and birds.

______

2 The frog stayed inside and tried to hide from the python.

______

3 Jason swam away from the crocodile and hoped it hadn't seen him.

______

4 A big moth flew around Mina's bedroom and made her very nervous.

______

[1] ecosystem ['i:kə,sɪstəm] *Ökosystem*

13 Holiday photos (Participle clauses) ➜ SB (p. 24) • GAP 17.1 (p. 74)

Match the sentence beginnings to the pictures. Then finish each sentence with a participle clause.

1 Here you can see my little sister at Manly Beach __________

2 Mark rested on a piece of wood __________

3 Brad and Rick sat on the car roof for a long time __________

14 While packing for their trip … (Participle clauses with *while* and *when*) ➜ SB (p. 25) • GAP 17.2 (p. 74)

Use participle clauses to join each pair of sentences. Start the participle clause with *while* or *when*.

1a) Tom's family packed for their trip to Australia.	1b) They got more and more excited.
2a) They found some cool places to stay.	2b) They looked online for information.
3a) They visited The Rocks.	3b) They spent hours at the markets.
4a) Tom fell off his board lots of times.	4b) He learned to surf.
5a) Emily lay on the beach at Cape Trib.	5b) She suddenly saw a cassowary.
6a) Some Germans took a wildlife tour with a guide.	6b) They spotted an amethyst python.
7a) One of the tourists filmed a river.	7b) He provoked a 6-metre-long crocodile.

1 *While packing for their trip to Australia, Tom's family got more and more excited.*

2 __________

3 __________

4 __________

5 __________

6 __________

7 __________

15 A terrible day at school ➜ SB (p. 25) • GAP 17 (p. 74)

○ Write a short text (about 150 words) in your exercise book about a bad day at school, using participle clauses. These ideas can help you get started:

ride bike to school – lose
art lesson: drop paint – make jeans very dirty
maths teacher: stand outside classroom – look angry
have English test – forget
chemistry lesson: do experiments – cause explosion
practise jumping at the gym – hurt

While riding my bike to school, I lost …

In the art lesson I dropped paint all over my legs, making …

16 Coming from Sydney … (Participle clauses to give reasons) ➜ *SB (p. 25) • GAP 18.1 (p. 75)*

Rewrite the sentences, using participle clauses to explain the reasons.

1 Brian and his family come from Sydney, which is why they find the weather in FNQ strange.

Coming from Sydney, Brian and his family find the weather in FNQ strange.

2 They hate wet weather, so they never go to FNQ between December and April.

____

3 Since Liz is from the Australian Capital Territory, she passed her driving test when she was 15.

____

4 Ava and Robin love to swim and surf, so they go to the beach as often as possible.

____

5 Ava has very light skin, which is why she has to put on a lot of sunscreen.

____

6 I'm interested in Australian culture, which is why I read a lot of books about it.

____

17 WORDS Nature in Australia ➜ *SB (p. 26) • Wordbanks 1–2*

You are going to work with words to help you talk about Australia's landscape and wildlife. Use your exercise book.

a) **Word field:** landscape and wildlife. Structure the vocabulary in the box, using a method you know (e. g. table, mind map, …). You can add more nouns.

> ant · bay · beach · bird · bush · camel · climate · coastline · coral reef · crocodile · flood · flying fox · inland · insect · kangaroo · koala · moth · mountain · ocean · outback · palm tree · python · rain · rainforest · region · river · rock · snake · spider · tree frog · wave · …

b) **Adjectives:** Look at the adjectives in the box. Find pairs that have opposite meanings, e. g. busy – remote.

> boring · busy · calm · coastal · cold · dangerous · deep · dry · exotic · flat · hot · humid · inland · lonely · marine · mild · mountainous · nearby · open · overcrowded · poisonous · relaxing · remote · rocky · rural · safe · sandy · scary · tiny · tropical · scenic · urban · vast · wet

c) **Verbs:** Which nouns from a) could you use before or after these verbs? Write sentences with your ideas.

> bite · bump into · flood · injure · provoke · swim

d) **Collocations:** Which adjectives from b) go well with these nouns? Find two or more possibilities for each noun.

> area · beach · city · landscape · ocean · plant · season

e) ● Prepare a page with pictures and a text for your class about Australia's landscape and wildlife. Before you start, make a list of twelve words or phrases that you want to use.

18 SPEAKING COURSE Agreeing and disagreeing → SB (p. 27) • SMC 18 (p. 82)

a) ○ Write three phrases you can use to give your opinion.

1 ____________ 2 ____________ 3 ____________

b) ○ Write three expressions you can use to agree with someone.

1 ____________ 2 ____________ 3 ____________

c) These three expressions are used to disagree with someone, but they are very direct. Write down different phrases or add extra phrases to make them more polite. (Look at step 3 on p. 27 of your student's book.)

1 That's nonsense. ____________

2 I don't agree. ____________

3 That's not how I see it. ____________

d) Think about the following statements and tick the correct sentences.

If you disagree with someone, you …

1 need to make your opinion clear, so you should start with a short answer like "No". ◯
2 should be very careful with expressions like "That's rubbish!" because they often seem rude. ◯
3 should remember that you can express your opinion even when you sound polite. ◯
4 will sound more polite if you're direct. ◯
5 should explain your opinion after you have given it. ◯
6 shouldn't show any understanding for the other person's opinion, because then your argument isn't clear. ◯

e) ● Write two arguments agreeing and two arguments disagreeing with each statement. Give reasons. Introduce your arguments with expressions from above or from p. 27 of your student's book. Use your arguments when discussing the statements in class.

1 "Towns would be much nicer if cars weren't allowed."
2 "Birds make better pets than cats or dogs."
3 "Money can't buy happiness."

____

____

____

____

____

____

____

____

19 EXTRA BACKGROUND FILE The Aboriginal people … ➔ SB (pp. 28–29)

a) Read the text and the timeline on pp. 28–29 of your student's book. Then tick the correct answers.

1 Australia's Aboriginal people …
- have always lived in Australia. ◯
- originally came from Asia. ◯
- originally came from Africa. ◯

2 The Aboriginal people …
- all spoke the same language. ◯
- spoke hundreds of languages or dialects. ◯
- wrote texts in many different languages. ◯

3 A songline is …
- a trail that is marked with hand-painted signs. ◯
- a kind of spiritual chant. ◯
- a path across the land recorded in a song. ◯

4 The songlines helped the Aboriginal people …
- to navigate the whole continent. ◯
- to build new roads and houses. ◯
- to cross the sea and explore new territories. ◯

b) Write down the answers.

1 How did the songlines help Aboriginal people to travel without maps? ______________________

____

____

2 Why did the Aboriginal population fall between 1788 and 1900? Give two reasons. ______________________

____

3 Who are the "Stolen Generations" and why were they given this name? ______________________

____

4 Name two events which show that a lot of Australians are sorry about the suffering of the Stolen Generations.

____

____

c) ● Look at the timeline again. Take notes about Aboriginal people's lives around 1900 and their lives today. Then use your notes to write a text of about 150 words in your exercise book.

	Around 1900	Today
population		
rights and opportunities		
social conditions		

20 Pintupi culture ➜ SB (p. 30)

○ Look at the text on p. 30 of your student's book again and read these statements. Tick T for true, F for false and N for not in the text.

	T	F	N
1 Pintupi is the name of a group of Aboriginal people and of the language they speak.	○	○	○
2 Coreen lives with her parents, her brothers and sisters, her grandparents and lots of other relatives.	○	○	○
3 When going out bush, the adults go hunting and the children look for goannas and witchety grubs.	○	○	○
4 The Pintupi go hunting because they eat a lot of meat.	○	○	○
5 During their time in the bush, Coreen's family is outside day and night.	○	○	○
6 "The Honey Ant dreaming" is a famous dreamtime story that Aboriginal people have told their children for hundreds of years.	○	○	○
7 Coreen's grandmother is also a successful artist who makes Aboriginal wall paintings for people's homes.	○	○	○
8 Coreen's class is quite small and not all the students attend school regularly.	○	○	○

21 WORDS Definitions ➜ SB (p. 31)

Complete the definitions with words from the text on p. 31 of your student's book.

1 The people who originally lived in a place before others arrived are called **i** ______________________ people.

2 If you think that someone is special or impressive, you **a** ________________ the person.

3 Someone who shows very strong feelings is **p** ____________________.

4 If you act or speak officially for a group of people and defend their interests, you **r** __________________ them.

5 The way you deal with people is your **t** ____________________ of them.

6 If you **u** ___________ other people to do something, you try hard to persuade them to do it.

7 You can **e** __________________ other people by helping them to achieve a goal.

8 People who are **o** ___________________ say exactly what they think, even if their opinions might shock others.

22 The Australian of the Year Awards ➜ SB (p. 32) • SMC 12 (p. 80)

a) ● 04 Listen to a German podcast about the Australian of the Year Awards. Write notes about:

- what the Australian of the Year Awards are
- when the winners receive their awards
- why the awards are important for Australia
- what kind of people win (including an example of what they do)
- what makes the awards unusual

b) Practise talking about the competition in English. Then give a one-minute talk to the class.

23 Life in Kintore (Past participle clauses) ➜ SB (p. 32) • GAP 18.2 (p. 75)

Rewrite the sentences with past participle clauses.

1 Kintore is a community that was founded in 1981, when many Pintupi people moved there from Papunya.

Kintore is a community founded in 1981, when many Pintupi people moved there from Papunya.

2 When the Pintupi were asked for a study what group they belonged to, 91 % of them said they were Aboriginal.

____

3 There is a group of artists from Kintore who are known for their special style of painting.

____

4 The paintings that are made by these artists sell for a lot of money.

____

5 Bush turkeys are just one kind of animal which are hunted by the Pintupi people when they go out bush.

____

6 "The Honey Ant dreaming" is a story that is told to Pintupi kids around the fire.

____

24 An Australian rock band (Present and past participle clauses) ➜ SB (p. 32) • GAP 17, 18 (pp. 74–75)

Fill in the correct participle: present or past.

1 Midnight Oil were an Australian rock band, originally ______________ (perform) under the name "Farm".

2 When ______________ (study) in Canberra, singer Peter Garret joined "Farm" – and the rest is history.

3 To choose their new name, the band wrote ideas on pieces of paper and put them in a hat, ______________ (pull out) "Midnight Oil" by chance.

4 The band sang about Kintore in "Beds are Burning", a song ______________ (describe) as the third-best Australian song ever.

5 "Beds are Burning" (1987) is a piece of music still ______________ (play) by radio stations all around the world today.

6 The band performed at the 2000 Sydney Olympics, ______________ (use) their show to raise awareness[1] of the suffering of Aboriginal people.

[1] awareness [əˈweənəs] *Bewusstsein*

1 WORDS Australia and the UK

Complete the sentences with words from this unit.

Australia and the UK have many things in common, even though they are very different countries – one ________ and ________, and the other small and, some might say, ________. The two countries share some of their history and culture because parts of Australia were ________ by British colonists, a lot of them ________. The colonists killed many ________ people whose terrible suffering has been recognised since the 1990s. Today there are many ________ between the UK and Australia. Young Brits or ________ can study or work in each other's country for a year or two. It's a very long ________ for them, but they can really profit from the opportunity. British people like the ________ way of life, the ________ landscapes and the ________ wildlife of Australia. Young Australians are interested in exploring the UK, with its ________ towns, ________ climate and famous ________.

2 AusE pronunciation

05 Listen and write the sentences.

1 ________________________________

2 ________________________________

3 ________________________________

4 ________________________________

3 A Brit in Sydney (Participle clauses)

Complete the text with the correct present and past participles. Use the verbs from the box.

ask · be · believe · cheer · clap · come · film · forget · help · pull · take · turn · visit · walk · *work*

Last summer Mark spent some time in Sydney *working* in a café. ________ British, he is allowed to work in Australia for two years. It's a café often ________ by tourists, so there are usually young people from all over the world ________ selfies in the street, ________ that cars in Australia drive on the left. Once, while ________ to work, Mark noticed two Spanish girls ________ each other in the road. Suddenly, he heard a car ________. The girls didn't look at it, ________ that they weren't in danger. Mark acted quickly, ________ them away from the road. People saw him ________ the girls. Soon, there was a crowd of people ________ and ________. Mark was embarrassed. The girls' video shows his face ________ red. But when ________ about it later by his boss, Mark felt quite proud.

4 What are they doing? (Listening for gist)

06 Listen to Olivia and her English friend Harry. What are they doing? Tick the right answers.

1 **A** ◯ Walking through flood water **B** ◯ Learning to surf **C** ◯ Taking a ferry to Manly

2 **A** ◯ Shopping in The Rocks **B** ◯ Watching an Australian Rules Football match **C** ◯ Going on a tour of Sydney CBD

5 A conversation at the beach (Listening for gist and detail)

a) 07 Listen to Megan, Finn and Zoe. What are they talking about? Circle A, B or C.

A A trip to England **B** Plans for an exchange year **C** Differences between Australia and the UK

b) 07 Read the questions. Then listen again and write short answers.

1 Which other cities will Finn travel through on his trip from Sydney to Glasgow? ______

2 How long will Finn's trip take? ______

3 Why does Megan think Finn will get a shock? ______

4 Why won't Finn miss his family? Give two reasons. ______

5 What will Finn miss most of all? ______

6 When was the host family's house built? ______

7 Why is Finn not sure if he understood everything the family told him? ______

8 Why does Zoe think the host parents might be strict? ______

9 What must Finn do in Glasgow? Name three things. ______

10 How many kilometres is Glasgow from Sydney? ______

Check: Listening

a) Vergleiche deine Antworten mit den Lösungen auf Seite 88 in diesem Workbook.
b) Schätze deine Antworten mit einem grünen oder roten Gesicht ein.

2 AusE pronunciation
Konntest du die Sätze in Aufgabe 2 ohne Probleme verstehen und aufschreiben? ◯ ◯ → 1

4 What are they doing?
Hast du in den Aufgaben 4/1 und 4/2 verstanden, was die Sprecher machen? ◯ ◯ → 3, 4a, 5a

5 A conversation at the beach
1 Hast du in 5a) problemlos verstanden, worüber sich die Freunde unterhalten? ◯ ◯ → 3, 4a, 5a
2 Konntest du in 5b) die Detailfragen ohne Probleme richtig beantworten? ◯ ◯ → 4b, 5b
3 Hast du in 5b) die Zahlen und Daten problemlos verstanden? ◯ ◯ → 2

c) Wenn du dich mit rot eingeschätzt hast, schau dir die rechte Spalte an.
Die Nummern führen dich zu den passenden Übungen im Skills Training (S. 16–17).
Dort kannst du gezielt Hören trainieren.

1 WORDS Understanding AusE ➜ SMC 21 (p. 83)

08 Listen and repeat the words and phrases you hear. Then write them down.

1 ____________ 6 ____________
2 ____________ 7 ____________
3 ____________ 8 ____________
4 ____________ 9 ____________
5 ____________ 10 ____________

TIP: Some words sound different in BE and AusE. Expect differences in words like these:
- light, look, leave
- letter, butter
- price, why, night
- stairs, care, where
- village, women
- next, pet, send
- cart, star, afternoon
- tea, seat

2 Numbers ➜ SMC 21 (p. 83)

09 Listen and write down the numbers.

1 ____________ 4 ____________ 7 ____________
2 ____________ 5 ____________ 8 ____________
3 ____________ 6 ____________ 9 ____________

TIP: Remember:
- 86 = **eighty**-six
- thir**teen** (13),
- thir**ty** (30)
- 2001: two thousand and one

3 Radio programmes (Listening for gist) ➜ SMC 21 (p. 83)

10 Noah is deciding which radio programmes to listen to. What are they about? Read the topics. Then listen once. Write the number of the programme (1–4) in the correct box.

- [ ] Young people leaving school
- [ ] "Australian of the Year" ceremonies
- [ ] Animals from around the world
- [ ] Job advice for teenagers
- [ ] Life without the Internet
- [ ] People who've done something great
- [ ] Helping Australian wildlife
- [ ] Teenagers who don't use technology

TIP: Listen only once for **gist (**the **general meaning),** not for details. Ask yourself **what the dialogue is about.** Look at the topics. Which words would you expect to hear? Listen for those **keywords.**

For example:
Animals from around the world → countries, live, feed

4 An Australian animal (Listening for gist and detail) ➜ SMC 21 (p. 83)

a) 11 Which animal are the people talking about? Listen once. Then circle A, B, C or D.

A crocodile

B cassowary

C bush turkey

D camel

b) 11 Read the statements. Then listen again. Tick T for true or F for false.

	T	F
1 Adult animals of this kind can be more than two metres tall.	◯	◯
2 If the baby animal was provoked, it would attack.	◯	◯
3 These animals use their toes to defend themselves.	◯	◯
4 These animals can run at 50 km/hour, but they can't swim.	◯	◯
5 These animals are nervous around humans.	◯	◯
6 These animals are vegetarian.	◯	◯
7 At the zoo they are fed fruit.	◯	◯
8 The modern world can be dangerous for these animals.	◯	◯
9 Dogs sometimes attack them.	◯	◯
10 In Queensland people are working to help these animals.	◯	◯

TIP: Find and mark **keywords** and **key phrases** in the statements. Then listen for them or for similar expressions when you listen a second time. Check numbers and dates carefully.

5 Tourist tips (Listening for gist and detail) ➔ *SMC 21 (p. 83)*

TIP: Before you listen, look at the **pictures.** They can help you understand the situation more easily.

a) 12 What is the conversation about? Listen once. Then circle A, B or C.

A Tours of The Rocks B Tours of Sydney C Photography tours

b) 12 Read the questions. Then listen again and write short answers.

TIP:
1 Before you listen a second time, mark **keywords** in the questions. Then listen for those words or words that have have a similar meaning.
2 Don't write sentences. Only write notes.

1 Who does Tim know from Perth? ______

2 How many hours does it take to drive from Perth to Sydney? ______

3 How many countries in the world are larger than Australia? ______

4 Why isn't Tim staying in Woolloomooloo? ______

5 What kind of areas does Tim like to visit when he is travelling? ______

6 How did he learn to use his camera? ______

7 What is special about the architect tours? ______

8 What does the building at 1 Bligh Street do with its used water? ______

9 Why does Tim think the price of the Manly bike tour is good? ______

10 Why would Aiden prefer the architect tour? ______

The Northeast of England

1 Impressions of the Northeast ➔ SB (pp. 40–41)

Look at the photos on pp. 40–41 in your student's book and at the photos on this page. What are your impressions of the Northeast of England? Make notes about nature/the environment, the economy and living/working conditions.

nature/the environment:

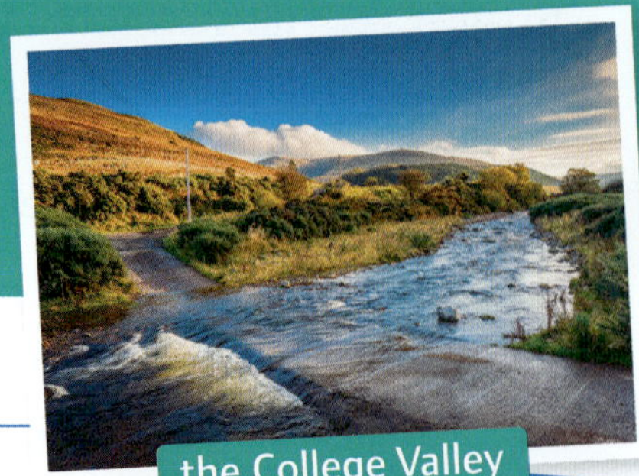
the College Valley

Durham

an old coal mine in Stanley

a wind farm in Teesside

the Central Arcade in Newcastl

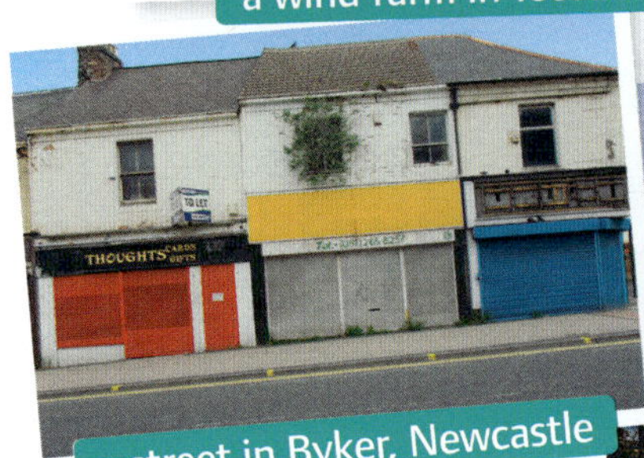
a street in Byker, Newcastle

Northumbria University

2 Serious or ironic? ➔ SB (p. 43)

13 Listen to three dialogues. Tick if the speakers' statements below are serious or ironic.

Situation	Statement	Serious	Ironic
1: In a museum	"Yes, Dad, I'm really excited I finally get to see these great pieces of art."	◯	◯
2: In a clothes shop	"Wow, it looks incredibly good on you."	◯	◯
3: At the dinner table	"What a fantastic idea to make a dish with all the food that's left in the house."	◯	◯

3 REVISION Things to do in Durham City (Simple past or present perfect) ➜ SB (p. 44) • GAP 5.1 (p. 66)

Complete the dialogue with the correct form of the verbs in brackets: simple past or present perfect.

Dad: Oh, I *'ve eaten* (eat) so much. That vegan apple pie we ____________ (have) for dessert __________ (be) absolutely delicious.

Joy: I really ___________ (like) it too. Okay, where shall we go now? We _______ ___________________ (not be able) to enjoy the great weather so far because we ______________________ (be) inside buildings most of the time.

Dad: Well, I __________________ (not show) you the River Wear yet. Last night I ______________ (download) a map with a route for a three-mile riverside walk with beautiful views and places along the way that we _________________ (not see) yet. We could also hire[1] a rowing boat[2]. When Mum and I __________ (be) students, we sometimes _____________ (spend) weekend afternoons on the river.

Joy: Why _______________________________ (we / never go) rowing in Newcastle?

Dad: Well, because that's by far not as special as it is in Durham. Here you can go through the heart of the city. It's a great free-time activity. I ____________________________ (really miss) it sometimes.

Joy: Both your ideas sound nice, but I'd prefer to hire a boat. It seems like fun.

4 REVISION Where did you go in the holidays? (Simple past) ➜ SB (p. 44) • GAP 2.1 (p. 64)

○ Write short dialogues in the simple past with the phrases.

1 where/you/go/in the holidays? – we/go/to the Northeast of England/for a few days

Where did you go in the holidays? – We went to the Northeast of England for a few days.

2 who/recommend/that destination/to you? – my parents' best friends/say/that/it/be/great

____

3 which places/you/visit? – we/visit/Newcastle and Durham

____

4 why/you/not send/me/any pictures? – because/I/forget

____

5 when/you/come back? – we/return/last Saturday

____

[1]hire [haɪə] *mieten* [2]rowing boat ['rəʊɪŋ ˌbəʊt] *Ruderboot*

5 REVISION A nice day trip (Simple past or past perfect) ➜ SB (p. 44) • GAP 2.1, 3.1 (pp. 64–65)

Make one sentence out of two. Connect the sentences with the words in brackets.
Use the past perfect for the earlier action.

1 Joy and her dad went to the students' residence. They looked at the library. (after)

Joy and her dad went to the students' residence after they had looked at the library.

2 Joy visited Durham Cathedral. She decided to watch some of the Harry Potter films again. (after)

After ______________________________

3 Joy and her dad ate lunch. They continued their tour of the city. (when)

____

4 On the way home they were very tired. They were active all day. (because)

____

5 Joy's father was a bit sentimental. He saw all the places from his student days again. (after)

____

6 Joy returned home. She sent her friends some nice photos of her day trip. (after)

____

6 What life used to be like in Newcastle (*used to* and *would*) ➜ SB (p. 45) • GAP 2.2 (p. 64)

Complete the sentences with *used to* or *would*.

1 In the 18th and 19th centuries, Newcastle __________ be a rich city.

2 At that time the shipyards and other heavy industries __________ need a lot of workers.

3 In the region around Newcastle, coal mines __________ dominate the landscape.

4 Even though the city was developing successfully, a lot of people __________ live in poverty.

5 Quite a few workers only __________ have jobs from spring to autumn and __________ suffer from hunger in winter.

6 Large numbers of children over ten years of age __________ work in the coal mines.

7 In the poor areas, little children __________ play in the dirty streets.

8 Although people who did not have any money usually could not go to hospital in 19th-century England, the Newcastle Infirmary[1] __________ provide[2] free treatment to a lot of the local poor.

[1]infirmary [ɪnˈfɜːmri] *Krankenhaus* [2]provide [prəˈvaɪd] *zur Verfügung stellen*

7 People's past habits (*used to* and *would*) ➜ SB (p. 45) • GAP 2.2 (p. 64)

Fill in *used to, didn't use to, would* or *wouldn't*.

1 When Mick was a child, he ________ hate spinach, but now he loves it.

2 For many years, Zoe ________________ switch the light off at night because she ________ be afraid of the dark.

3 In the 1960s, most British families ________________ travel to other countries in the summer, but ____________ stay at home or go camping at the seaside or in the countryside.

4 Until the 2000s, people ____________ go shopping in their local area because they couldn't buy things online yet.

5 When my grandparents were young, they ____________ be aware of environmental problems.

8 What did they use to do? (*used to* and *would*) ➜ SB (p. 45) • GAP 2.2 (p. 64)

a) Make questions with *used to* about people's past habits.

1 how/people/travel/one hundred years ago?

How did people use to travel one hundred years ago?

2 a lot of people/do sport/in the 19th century?

____

3 what/teenagers/do/in their free time/around 1900?

____

4 there/be/many concerts/in Newcastle/in the 1970s?

____

5 the Northeast/be/a popular tourist destination/fifty years ago?

____

TIP: You can ask questions about repeated actions and situations in the past by using **did + subject + use to**.

Examples:
Did Joy's parents use to spend a lot of time in the library as students?
Where did they use to have lunch?

You can also form questions with **did there use to be** if you want to find out about situations in the past.

Example:
Did there use to be any vegetarian restaurants in this town?

b) Match these answers with the questions from a).

A Yes, they did.
B Yes, there did.
C They used to go by train or ship.
D No, it didn't.
E They met with relatives or went to public events.

1	C	2		3		4		5	

9 How times have changed (*used to* and *would*) ➜ *SB (p. 45) • GAP 2.2 (p. 64)*

Use the information in the table to write about people's habits in the past and now.

In the past	Now
wash clothes by hand	have washing machines
call family and friends from public phones	use mobiles
find one's way with the help of maps	use GPS
write letters to stay in touch	send e-mails and text messages
look for information in encyclopedias[1]	do research on the internet

In the past, people used to/would wash clothes by hand, but now they have washing machines.

____

____

____

____

10 BACKGROUND FILE The Northeast of England ➜ *SB (pp. 46–47)*

a) ○ Read the text on pp. 46–47 of your student's book again. Then close the book and read these statements. Tick T for true and F for false.

	Statement	T	F
1	Newcastle-upon-Tyne is among the five largest cities in the UK.	○	○
2	The economy in the Northeast used to be dependent on heavy industries, but in the last few decades IT companies and other service industries have become more important parts of it.	○	○
3	In the early 20th century, the shipbuilding industry in Newcastle and other places in the Northeast produced half of the world's ships.	○	○
4	Coal mining in the Northeast started in medieval times.	○	○
5	In 1825, the first railway for passengers transported 40,000 people.	○	○
6	Newcastle and Gateshead used to be two cities, but nowadays they are one city.	○	○
7	The Venerable Bede, whose tomb is in Newcastle Cathedral, was an English king who wrote a famous history book.	○	○
8	Nowadays there are a lot of call centres in Newcastle because people think that the Geordie accent sounds really nice.	○	○

b) ● Read the text on pp. 46–47 of your student's book again and answer these questions in your exercise book.

1 What tourist attractions are there in the Northeast? Name at least five.

2 Which two inventions by George Stevenson are mentioned in the text and why were they important for the economy of the Northeast?

3 How is the Northeast trying to meet the challenges of the 21st century?

4 What is special about Geordies?

[1] encyclopedia [ɪnˌsaɪklə'piːdiə] *Lexikon, Enzyklopädie*

11 The Angel of the North ➔ SB (pp. 46–47) • SMC 12, 21 (pp. 80, 83)

You are going to travel to the Northeast of England with a youth group from your community. Each of you is asked to present information about one interesting sight to the group so you can decide together which places you want to visit.

a) 14 The group leader has asked you to collect some information about the Angel of the North. Listen to the report from a travel radio show and take notes about reasons for visiting this sight.

____

____

____

____

____

____

____

____

____

b) Use your notes to give a short talk in German to the youth group about the Angel of the North. Say if you think it is worth visiting and give reasons.

12 REVISION Let's go to a café, shall we? (Making suggestions and offers: *can, could, shall*)

➔ SB (p. 50) • GAP 11 (p. 70)

Complete the suggestions and offers with *can, could* or *shall*.

In town

Grandmother: Let's go to a café, *shall* we? I'd love a piece of cake.

Sue: Great idea, Gran, but __________ I have ice cream instead of cake, please?

At the cinema

Sinan: __________ you find the seats while I get us some popcorn?

Oscar: Sure. __________ you also get me a bottle of water?

Sinan: Okay. __________ I get a small or a large one?

At Durham Cathedral

Tourist: Excuse me, __________ we have two audio guides, please?

Visitor desk assistant: I'm sorry, we don't have audio guides. But you __________ book a guided tour if you like.

Tourist (to his wife): What do you think, Megan? __________ we take the tour?

13 REVISION Could you …? (Asking people to do things: *can, could, would*) ➜ SB (p. 50) • GAP 11 (p. 70)

a) ○ Read the descriptions of different situations. Tick the best request for each situation.

You enter a café. You can't get to the only free table because a woman has put a huge shopping bag on the floor.	"Hello, can you move that bag, please?"	○
	"Excuse me, could I ask you to move your bag, please?"	○
	"I can't get to the free table. Would you please move your bag?"	○
Your best friend has come over to your place and you have prepared some snacks. You can't carry everything to your room at the same time and ask him or her for help.	"Can you take the nuts and crisps?"	○
	"Do you think you could take the nuts and crisps?"	○
	"Would you be able to take the nuts and crisps?"	○
You are staying with a British host family and you are watching TV together. The window is open and you feel very cold.	"It's getting a bit cold in here. Shall I close the window?"	○
	"Sorry, it's really cold in here. Can I close the window?"	○
	"Sorry, but do you think I could close the window?"	○

b) Write requests for these situations in your exercise book.

1 You don't have a ruler and would like to use your partner's.
2 You don't remember how to use the past perfect and decide to ask your English teacher for help.
3 You are taking part in a discussion and can't follow one person's arguments.

14 You should turn off your computer (*should, shouldn't, ought to*) ➜ SB (p. 51) • GAP 11 (p. 70)

a) Fill in *should, shouldn't* or *ought to*.

Mother: It's late, Evie. You *should* turn off your computer.

Evie: But, Mum, I really ________ finish this presentation today.

Mother: How many times have I told you that you ________ leave your assignments until the last minute?
You've probably had enough time for this presentation and ________ be working now.

Evie: I know I ________ be better organised.

Mother: You have to get up at 6:30 so you ________ be in bed by 10:30 at the very latest. You ________ have another half hour. A fifteen-year-old ________ get at least eight hours of sleep.

b) Read the advice. Underline the parts that sound unfriendly or even rude. Then rewrite them using *I think/don't think* to make them sound more polite.

1 Archie is really sad. Tell him you're sorry. ________
2 You'll do fine on the exam. Don't worry so much. ________
3 Don't work all day. You look very tired. ________
4 Oh dear, you're not very fit. You ought to exercise more. ________
5 You shouldn't care what people say. You're wonderful! ________

15 WORDS Relationships and feelings ➜ SB (p. 52) • Wordbank 4

You are going to revise words which you can use to talk about relationships and feelings.
Then you will prepare a one-minute talk for your class about the relationship between people in a photo.

a) **Word field:** relationships. Choose at least five phrases and explain their meaning. Write in your exercise book.

break up (with sb.) · go out with sb. · be attracted to sb. · fall in love (with sb.) · make friends · give sb. a second chance · get to know sb. · be seeing sb. · get married · get back together · be friendly with sb. · date sb. · be furious with/at sb.

When you break up with somebody, you end the relationship with them.

b) **Adjectives:** feelings. Make as many pairs of opposites as you can with words from the box. Sometimes you can link a word with more than one other word. For some words there will be no opposites.

afraid · angry · annoyed · bored · calm · confident · confused · cross · disappointed · excited · frightened · furious · glad · glum · happy · heartbroken · hopeful · nervous · optimistic · pessimistic · pleased · relaxed · sad · scared · shocked · shy · terrified · thrilled · unhappy · upset · worried

bored – excited	______	______
______	______	______
______	______	______
______	______	______

c) **Collocations and compounds:** relationships. Choose one word from each box to complete the sentences.

family · *ex-* (2x) · new · best · true

acquaintance · boyfriend · friend (2x) · mate · *wife*

1 Steve still misses his *ex-wife* even though they got divorced three years ago.

2 Marcus often has dinner with us on Sundays. He's an old ______.

3 I made a ______ at the gym last month. His name's Abdullah.

4 Tom is Ella's ______. He's now seeing Nadira.

5 When I have problems, Vanessa always listens and tries to support me. She's a ______.

6 James hangs out with William a lot. He's his ______.

d) ● Choose a photo of people who have a special relationship. They can be people you know, e.g. family or friends, or people you admire, e.g. famous actors, singers or influencers. You could also use one of the photos above. Prepare a one-minute talk for your class in which you describe the people's relationship. Before you start, make a list of 8–10 words and phrases from a)–c) that you want to use.

16 REVISION You must be excited (*must be/can't be; must have been/can't have been*)

SB (p. 55) • GAP 11.1 (p. 70)

a) Write what person B could say in the following situations. Use *must be* or *can't be* with a word from the box.

easy · excited · furious · lonely · serious

1 **A:** Beatrice wants to go out with me! She's the girl of my dreams! – **B:** You must be excited.

2 **A:** Some of my friends posted some really silly photos of me. – **B:** You ______.

3 **A:** I'm taking Japanese classes after school twice a week. – **B:** That ______.

4 **A:** Our neighbour's dog barks all day when nobody is at home. – **B:** That dog ______.

5 **A:** I read 20 books last month! All of them were fantastic. – **B:** You ______.

b) Complete the sentences. Use *must have* or *can't have* with the past participle of the verbs in brackets.

1 There should be some pizza left. Joe ______ it all! (eat)

2 Melanie told Jacob she didn't love him anymore. He ______ so upset. (be)

3 The Angel of the North is an amazing piece of art. It ______ quite long to build it. (take)

4 Zoe thinks she saw Ahmed in town yesterday, but she ______ him because he was ill in bed. (see)

5 Grandma didn't send me a birthday card. She ______. (forget)

6 Mum and Dad ______ to bed yet because all the lights are still on. (go)

17 It might happen, but who knows? (*may* and *might*)

SB (p. 55) • GAP 11 (p. 70)

a) Read the tip.

b) Add some information to these statements that shows how likely the event is.

1 Marian may go to Australia for a year. ______

______

2 Marian might go to Australia for a year. ______

______

TIP: You use both **may** and **might** to express a possibility. There is only a small difference between them. You could say that *may* expresses a possibility of about 50 per cent, whereas a statement with *might* indicates that something is less certain.

Examples:
Brenda and I may go out tonight, but we're not sure.
Our school's football team hasn't been very strong this season but they might win the match today.

c) Complete the sentences with *may* or *might* and the verbs from the box.

be · not be · move · need · surprise

1 Mona ______ soon. Her parents are looking for new jobs.

2 This building looks like a ruin, but it ______ too late to save it.

3 It's really late so it ______ difficult to find an open restaurant in this small village.

4 I'm getting on really well with my assignment at the moment, but I ______ some help later on.

5 It ______ you that Vicky has become a vegetarian as she used to eat so much meat.

18 Interpreting a cartoon ➜ SB (p. 56)

a) Look at the cartoon and describe the situation.

"After using the Internet all day, Brad doesn't like any kind of popup."

b) What is the reason for the man's reaction?

c) What is the message of the cartoon? What is funny about it?

d) Compare your answers in class.

19 Influencer – a great job? ➜ SB (p. 56) • SMC 8, 21 (pp. 78, 83)

a) 15 Listen to a radio report. What is the difference between influencers Elliott and Nicola? Write one sentence.

b) Listen again and take notes in your exercise book about …

1 the content of Elliott's vlogs (three examples)
2 the number of Elliott's followers
3 how much money mid-level influencers get per post
4 the main content of Nicola's posts
5 the number of Nicola's followers
6 how much money micro-influencers get per post
7 what parents and journalists criticize about influencers
8 what social media specialist Candice Burton says about influencers.

c) Can influencers be role models for young people? Write an argumentative text in your exercise book. Look at p. 21 of your student's book for help.

20 STUDY SKILLS Kids' online behaviour ➔ *SB (p. 57) • SMC 26 (p. 84), Wordbank 5*

a) Look at the chart and make notes on the questions below in your exercise book.

Devices used by children aged 10 to 15 years to go online, England and Wales, year ending March 2020

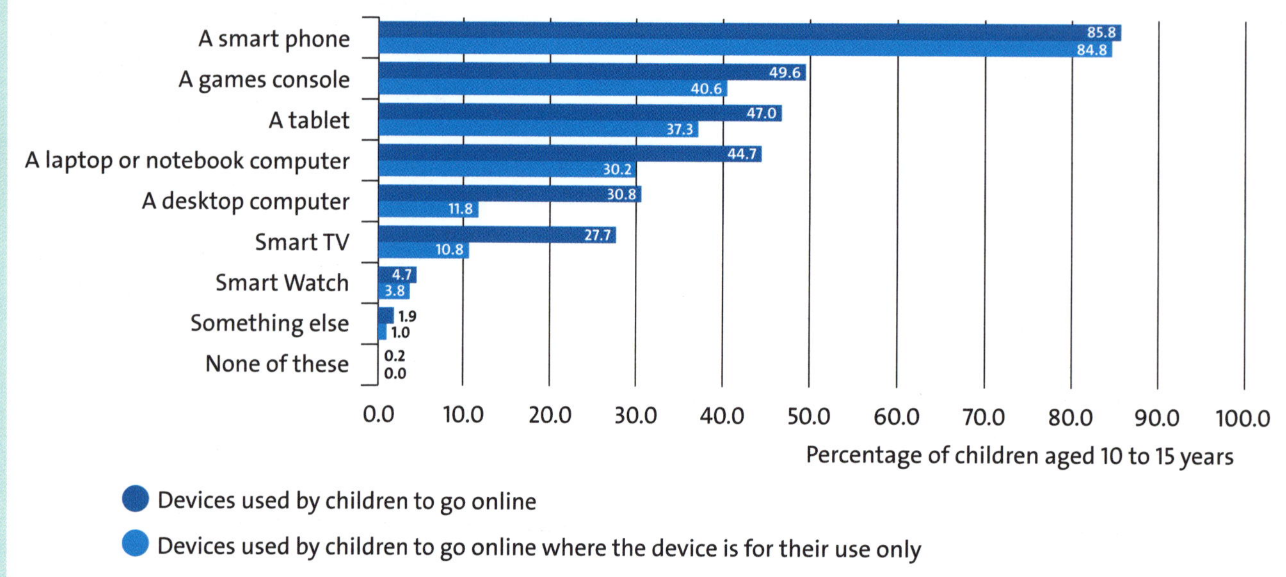

Source: *UK Office for National Statistics; Release date: 9 February 2021*

Notes: Percentages may not sum to 100 as respondents may have given more than one answer.

Owning portable[1] devices such as smart phones and laptops gives children the ability to go online from anywhere. While almost all children (98 %) said they went online or used the internet at home, many children went online in other places such as in a friend or relative's home (59 %), at school or college as part of a lesson (55 %), or when they were on their way somewhere (42 %).

1 What do you call this way of presenting statistics?
2 What information does it give you (what, who, where, when)?
3 Why are there two bars for each device?
4 What is the reason for the different percentages in the two bars for each device?
5 What general conclusions can you draw from this chart at first sight (children's internet use, their favourite devices, devices available per child)?

b) Look at the details of the statistics and complete the statements.

1 ________ per cent of the children who were interviewed had a smart phone for their use only.

2 ________ per cent used a desktop computer, while only ________ per cent of them owned such a device.

3 37.3 per cent of the children had their own ____________________.

4 Almost 50 per cent ____________ a games console to go online and ________ per cent owned such a device.

5 10.8 per cent had their own smart TV while about three times as many had ______________________________.

c) Write at least five more statements like in b) in your exercise book.

d) What are the most interesting facts that you have learned from the statistics? Make notes.

____

____

e) ● Use your answers from a)–d) to prepare a short talk for your class. You could also record yourself.

[1]portable ['pɔːtəbl] *tragbar, portabel*

21 SPEAKING COURSE Having a discussion ➜ SB (p. 59) • SMC 17 (p. 81)

You are going to prepare a discussion about this statement:

The internet has more advantages than disadvantages.

a) Note down your first ideas about the statement.

b) In a group, compare your ideas and write all your arguments in the table below.
Have you collected more or less the same number of arguments for each list?
If not, try to come up with more points.

Arguments for the statement	Arguments against the statement

c) Write "for" and "against" on small pieces of paper. You need as many pieces of paper as there are students in your class and equal numbers of "for"s and "against"s. Put them in a bag or a box. Each of you draws one piece so you know which position you have to take in the discussion.

d) Look at the arguments that you want to use in the discussion. Think of good examples to support them.

e) Form new groups of four and have a discussion. Two people present arguments for the statement and two present arguments against it.
Before you start, look at the steps on page 59 of your student's book again.
Use the phrases which you revised on that page.

f) Compare your conclusions in class.

1 WORDS Learning to deal with money

Complete the text with words from this unit.

In 2021, kids in the UK on average got almost £12 a week in pocket money. Some had to earn it by doing different jobs and household __________. Having to ______________ helps them to appreciate the __________ of money. Of course, they won't always spend their pocket money wisely from the beginning and will sometimes ______________ __________ it before the end of the month. But they will learn to __________________ their needs and their wants. Parents should tell their children clearly which ______________ they expect them to meet with their pocket money. They should also ____________________ them to save for something special. Younger kids can put a certain amount into a ____________________ each month, while teenagers can open their first bank ______________.

2 Some tips on how to stay safe online *(should, shouldn't, ought to)*

Fill in *should, shouldn't* or *ought to*.

1 You ______________ post photos of other people without asking them if they agree to it.

2 You ____________________ use strong passwords with letters, numbers and symbols.

3 You ____________________ report people who do illegal things online.

4 You ______________ give people you don't know your bank details.

3 Hadrian's Wall – history and attractions

a) You want to find out why Hadrian's Wall was built. Skim the text. Mark the paragraph in which you might find the information.

Hadrian's Wall, which is located in northern England, is one of Europe's greatest ancient monuments. Almost 120 kilometres long, three metres wide and five metres high, it is an impressive landmark. It runs between Wallsend on the River Tyne and Bowness-on-Solway on the Irish Sea.

The wall was built during a time when large parts of Britain belonged to the Romans. The Emperor Hadrian decided that such a border would make it easier to control his territories. After it had been built, people could probably only enter the empire at certain points and then travel to markets or other places, accompanied by military. The wall also made the Roman Empire safer as it was often attacked on its borders.

Setting up the wall was a huge task. Between the years 122 and 128, many thousands of soldiers were ordered to build the stone structure and also towers, forts and bridges.

Much of Hadrian's Wall is still there and has been a UNESCO World Heritage Site since 1987. You can discover the whole monument on the Hadrian's Wall Path, which was opened in 2003. Along the way you can visit museums, Roman forts, milecastles, turrets, temples and even an ancient bath house.

b) Scan the text to find the answers to the questions below. Mark the information.

1 How long did it take to build Hadrian's Wall?

2 If you want to visit the whole monument, where can you start and where do you arrive? (two possibilities)

4 The rise and fall of the British coal industry

a) First mark keywords in the questions. Then scan the text and answer the questions in your exercise book. Try to use your own words.

1 What was coal used for in the Industrial Revolution?
2 How important were the coalfields in the Northeast?
3 Where and why did new towns appear?
4 What caused the decline of the British coal industry?
5 Why has the situation improved now?
6 Summarize the statements in the report from 2019.

Today the world has to find alternatives to using coal because of its high CO_2 emissions. The use of this fossil fuel increased during the Industrial Revolution when it became one of the most important sources of energy.

Coal mining in the 19th and early 20th centuries

During the Industrial Revolution, coal was needed to produce steel and to power locomotives, steamships and machines in factories. It was also widely used to heat houses. There were coalfields in many parts of Britain where millions of tons were mined every year. Two important ones, the Durham and Northumberland coalfields, were located in the Northeast of England. By 1913, about 25 per cent of Britain's coal was produced in this region. Miners' homes were built near the pits and so new towns appeared in which almost the whole population lived from mining.

The decline of the coal industry

By the mid-20th century, the British coal industry was in decline as it was cheaper to buy coal from abroad or use other sources of energy. Moreover, steam railways were replaced by diesel and electric trains. Private households switched to central heating and from the late 1980s, there was increased awareness of the environmental problems caused by burning coal.

The effects on the population

The closures of the coal mines caused extreme difficulties because a lot of ex-miners were unable to find new work. By now, the situation has greatly improved because jobs in modern industries have been created. Nonetheless, an official report from 2019 stated that mining towns and villages across the UK had still not completely recovered. Not only ex-miners, but the population of the former mining towns as a whole suffers from problems such as unemployment, ill health and social disadvantage.

b) What do the underlined words and phrases mean? Guess from the context. If you aren't sure, look them up. Write the translations in your exercise book. (Use the infinitives of the verb forms.)

Check: Reading

a) Vergleiche deine Antworten mit den Lösungen auf Seite 88 in diesem Workbook.
b) Schätze deine Antworten mit einem grünen oder roten Gesicht ein.

	☺	☹	
3 Hadrian's Wall – history and attractions			
1 Konntest du in 3a) durch *skimming* den richtigen Absatz finden?	○	○	→ 1
2 Konntest du in 3b) durch *scanning* schnell die richtigen Antworten finden?	○	○	→ 3a–b
4 The rise and fall of the British coal industry			
1 Konntest du in 4a) wichtige *keywords/phrases* in den Fragen erkennen?	○	○	→ 3a
2 Konntest du mithilfe deiner *keywords/phrases* die Fragen beantworten?	○	○	→ 3b
3 Konntest du in 4b) die Wörter leicht erschließen oder schnell nachschlagen?	○	○	→ 2

c) Wenn du dich mit rot eingeschätzt hast, schau dir die rechte Spalte an. Die Nummern führen dich zu den passenden Übungen im Skills Training (S. 32–33). Dort kannst du gezielt das Lesen trainieren.

1 Different types of friendship ➜ SMC 1 (p. 76)

Skim the text. What is it about? Circle A, B or C.

A the negative effects of social media on relationships

B a comparison of the value of online and real-life friendships

C tips on how to find friends on the internet and in real life

TIP:
1 You **skim** to find out the main information in a text, not details. What does the whole text tell you about?
2 You **scan** to find details in part of the text with the help of keywords.

Most of us communicate online with friends and there are quite a few among them that we only contact on social media. So does it really make a differererence whether we foster friendships virtually or face-to-face?

Great things about online friendships
Social media provide lots of opportunities to meet interesting people. You chat with a friend's friend, the person seems nice, and you add them to your contacts. Soon you will have a large network of friends you can get in touch with when you are bored or want to exchange ideas. Whether you're a sci-fi fan or a hobby photographer, it's never been easier to find like-minded people. Online friends may gradually even become quite close and help each other with personal problems.

Qualities only real-life friendships have
However, a lot of fun things are only possible in the real world: having a good time together at the cinema, eating out, doing sports or just hanging out in your room for hours. Only real-life friends throw a surprise party for you on your birthday and bring you little presents when you are ill. They know that you're depressed just by looking at you and can console you in a way that no online friend ever could. They won't pretend to be someone they're not whereas on the internet people often only show their best self and can easily deceive you. An online friend may sometimes give you useful advice, but your best friend in the real world knows you better and will tell you the truth even if it's painful.

Finding a good balance
Today, online friendships are as much a part of a digital native's world as friendships in real life. Using social media can definitely enrich our relationships and make our lives more exciting. Teenagers in particular find it easy to develop friendships online and enjoy being in touch with a large number of people. There is nothing wrong with that. The question is rather what importance we give to our virtual connections and if we can find a good balance and foster both kinds of friendships. Online friendships can be a valuable addition to our social interaction, but they can never replace our contacts with people in the real world – people we can trust and rely on.

2 What does it mean? ➜ SMC 2 (p. 76)

Mark these words in exercise 1. Then find the correct meanings. Use an English-German dictionary only if necessary.

TIP: Before you use a dictionary:
– Think about the **context**. What makes sense?
– Is there a **similar German word**?
– Do you know a **similar English, French or Latin word**? Or one from another language?
– Look for clues in the **context** of the sentence.
If you need a dictionary, **read all the meanings** of the word and choose the one that fits the context.

1 foster: ______________________

2 provide: ______________________

3 like-minded: ______________________

4 gradually: ______________________

5 console: ______________________

6 deceive: ______________________

7 painful: ______________________

8 enrich: ______________________

9 replace: ______________________

10 rely on sb.: ______________________

3 Influencers with serious messages ➔ SMC 1–2 (p. 76)

a) First read the questions in b). Then scan the text for the answers.

> **TIP:** Mark keywords in the questions and look for them or for similar words when you scan the text. Then read around the keywords to find the answers. Look at the example.

Some influencers on social media are modern-day superstars. They give beauty, fashion and food tips; show us workouts and how to play the latest video games; or travel to amazing places. They seem to live in a perfect world and the most successful ones among them make quite a lot of money because companies pay them for using and advertising their products. Sales[1] often increase by up to 30 % due to recommendations by popular role models on social media. However, not all influencers only care about shopping and having fun. In recent years a new type has become increasingly popular: the purpose-driven[2] influencers.

Different messages

Purpose-driven influencers inform their followers about ways to save the environment by buying "green" products, reducing waste[3], doing without plastics and supporting animal rights. They say that they only post about a product if they agree with the idea behind it. Some of them are also politically active or support social movements against discrimination and racism.

Reaching young people

Studies show that especially 14 to 19-year-olds trust influencers more than traditional advertisers and therefore like to buy the products their role models recommend. As more and more young people are worried about climate change, they also want to find out about environmentally-friendly products and specifically listen to advice from purpose-driven influencers. Because of this trend, a lot of companies have become interested in working together with these influencers to get a greener image.

Really different from the others?

So are purpose-driven influencers in fact not that different from other influencers? They are criticized for several reasons. After all, they are dependent on marketing too. Certain messages also don't make sense. For instance, some of the influencers say that vegan food is the best choice even though the production of large numbers of plants such as soya leads to environmental problems in other parts of the world. In addition, informing people about a green way of life shouldn't just be about better shopping habits, but also about buying much less.

Fake and real purpose-driven influencers

It makes sense to watch out for influencers on social media who only want to make a profit by pretending to be green, but don't offer reliable facts. Real purpose-driven influencers need to make money too, but that's not their focus. Their main content is about sustainability[4], not about themselves. They give shopping tips, but they also show how to re-use and repair things or encourage followers to buy second-hand items. People like this want to set an example and present a way of life that will bring about some positive changes.

b) Answer the questions in your exercise book in your own words.

1 What do companies pay influencers for?
2 How much do sales increase if influencers advertise products?
3 What do purpose-driven influencers tell their followers about?
4 What age group listens to influencers rather than to traditional advertisers?
5 Why are more and more companies becoming interested in working together with purpose-driven influencers?
6 For what reasons are purpose-driven influencers sometimes criticized?
7 What are some differences between fake and real purpose-driven influencers?

> **TIP:**
> 1 If you can't find a keyword, look for a similar word or phrase, e. g. 'tell' is the same as 'inform'. Sometimes you also have to look for a word that is connected to a phrase in the question, e. g. 'old' is connected to 'age group'.
> 2 If the question asks 'How much/many …' look for numbers and also the per cent sign (%).
> 3 Remember that a verb may be in a different tense in the text: e. g. 'are becoming' in the question may be 'have become' in the text.

[1]sales [seɪlz] *Umsatz* [2]purpose-driven ['pɜːpəsˌdrɪvn] *zweckorientiert* [3]waste ['weɪst] *Abfall* [4]sustainability [səˌsteɪnə'bɪləti] *Nachhaltigkeit*

The Southwest of the USA

1 Places in the Southwest ➜ SB (p. 68) • SMC 21 (p. 83)

a) 16 A Canadian class is looking at different regions of the USA. One student gives a presentation about places in the Southwest. Match the photos with the names. Then listen and check your answers.

- ◯ Humboldt-Toiyabe National Forest, Nevada
- ◯ Salt Lake City, Utah
- ◯ White Sands, New Mexico
- ◯ Aspen, Colorado
- (1) Grand Canyon National Park, Arizona

b) Find the places on a map.

c) Look up these words and write down their German meaning.

World Heritage Site – ______________________ gypsum – ______________________

dune – ______________________ Mormon – ______________________

d) Listen again and write down three interesting facts about each place.

____

____

____

____

____

____

____

____

2 American and British schools ➔ SB (p. 71)

a) Read the text on p. 71 of your student's book again. Then tick T for true, F for false and N for not in the text.

	T	F	N
1 The US government is responsible for the high school system.	◯	◯	◯
2 For town and city kids, driving is not the usual method of getting to school.	◯	◯	◯
3 US students study more subjects in grade 10 than in grades 11 and 12.	◯	◯	◯
4 25% of US students' grade for the year come from end-of-year exams.	◯	◯	◯
5 In the UK, comprehensive schools are state-run and grammar schools are private.	◯	◯	◯
6 American public schools are state-run, but British public schools are not.	◯	◯	◯
7 Lessons usually start earlier in the UK than in the US.	◯	◯	◯
8 At the end of Year 9 typical British students complete their GCSE exams.	◯	◯	◯
9 The two school years of sixth form are called Lower Sixth and Upper Sixth.	◯	◯	◯

b) ● Write five more statements about the different school systems. Your partner has to say if they are true, false or not in the text.

3 REVISION Historical facts about schools in the US (The passive) ➔ SB (p. 72) • GAP 9, 10.1 (pp. 68–69)

Fill in the passive forms of the verbs in brackets. Pay attention to the tenses.

the first high school in Chicago, 1800s

1 The first American public school *was founded* (found) in Boston in 1635.

2 By the mid-19th century a lot of schools ______________________ (set up) everywhere in New England and had replaced homeschooling.

3 Most children of rich people in the South, however, ______________ (tutor) at home by private teachers or they ______________ (send) to private schools.

4 By 1910, about 72 per cent of American children ______________ (teach) in schools.

5 Even though the American Constitution states that "all men ______________________ (create) equal", African American children ______________________ (segregate), which meant that they had to go to separate schools.

6 After these children ______________________________________ (discrimate against) by school laws for a long time, the Civil Rights Movement helped to bring about the end of segregation in education.

7 Homeschooling ______________________________ (consider) a better form of education than public schooling by a growing number of American parents in recent years.

8 It looks like the K-12 system ______________________ (change) within the next decade to include more computer skills and foreign languages in academic training.

4 A visit to Santa Fe (Passive of verbs with two objects: simple past) ➜ *SB (p. 72)* • *GAP 10.2 (p. 69)*

Sandy and Louise, two girls from New York, visited Santa Fe.
Rewrite their statements using the personal passive.
First underline the verb that you have to change.

TIP: In passive sentences, you can leave out the information about who did something.

1 We stayed at the International Youth Hostel where they gave us a simple but clean room.

We stayed at the International Youth Hostel where we were given a simple but clean room.

2 Some friendly local people told us about the history of Santa Fe when we visited the Old Town.

____

3 We also booked a walking tour of the city and the guide showed our tourist group some great historic sites.

____

4 We went to some markets where people offered us typical Southwestern things.

____

5 They asked us to clean our room before we left the hostel.

____

5 My mom has been offered a job (Passive of verbs with two objects: present perfect) ➜ *SB (p. 73)* • *GAP 10.2 (p. 69)*

Complete the sentences with the verbs in brackets. Use the present perfect form of the personal passive.

1 My mom *has been offered* (offer) a job in Arizona, but we aren't sure if we want to move there.

2 Yolanda ______________ (promise) a big party for her 16th birthday.

3 Miguel and José have been working at a café for two months, but they ______________ (not pay) their wages[1] yet.

4 Jason ______________ (just tell) a strange story about his best friend that he simply can't believe.

5 We ______________ (not give) the opportunity to meet students from other countries so far.

6 The Morenos ______________ (send) lots of parcels from Mexico recently.

[1] wage [weɪdʒ] *Lohn*

6 WORDS Describing people and feelings ➜ *SB (p. 74) • Wordbank 4*

a) Write the missing words in the table. Use a dictionary to find the words you don't know.

Adjective (negative)	Adjective (positive)	Noun (positive)
unfair	fair	*fairness*
	possible	
	patient	
	kind	
	dependent	

Adjective (negative)	Adjective (positive)	Noun (positive)
	similar	
	regular	
	reliable	
	relevant	
	available	

b) Complete the sentences with some words from a).

1 English and Chinese are very different languages. They are completely ________________ from each other.

2 Don't give up! Doing difficult tasks always takes a great deal of ________________.

3 Expensive cars are ________________ to most people.

4 We needn't use this information in our presentation. I think it is ________________ to the topic.

5 If we want to stop climate change, we have to end our ________________ on coal, oil and gas.

c) Write at least three more sentences with words from a) in your exercise book.

7 EXTRA BACKGROUND FILE The Southwest ➜ *SB (pp. 76–77)*

a) Look at the text on pp. 76–77 of your student's book again. Tick the topics that are mentioned in the text.

- ◯ Population
- ◯ Climate
- ◯ Religion
- ◯ History and culture
- ◯ Famous people from the region
- ◯ Geography
- ◯ Wildlife
- ◯ Economy
- ◯ Regional food
- ◯ Current challenges

b) Read the statements. Tick the ones that are correct.

1 The US military needs land in the desert to practise fighting in hot and dry climates. ◯

2 The purpose of dams is to supply regions with water and to generate electricity. ◯

3 The old adobe houses in Taos Pueblo are empty ruins nowadays. ◯

4 Phoenix is older than Las Vegas, but younger than Santa Fe. ◯

5 Most of the Southwest first belonged to Mexico and later to Spain. ◯

8 ACCESS TO CULTURES High school students' community service
→ SB (p. 79) EN/DE

a) Read the article and underline any keywords and key phrases.

Nowadays, many US high schools have community service regulations[1]. In order to graduate[2], students have to spend a certain number of hours helping elderly or homeless people, supporting younger students, taking part in environmental projects, collecting things for charities or doing other tasks in their neighborhood. These requirements are supposed to make young people more conscious of the problems of others and help them develop the skills they need to become active and responsible citizens.

Policies vary[3] greatly between states and districts. While Maryland and the District of Columbia have state-wide regulations that require students to complete 75 to 100 hours of community service in order to graduate, the rules are different in other places. Often so-called service learning courses are mandatory[4], during which students discuss community issues in class and try to come up with solutions for them. Usually they have to put their ideas into practice and afterwards receive credits for their projects.

The introduction of mandatory volunteering has led to some protest. Quite a few parents, students, and even school officials are against community service policies, arguing that activities in the community should not be another form of homework. Kids should be able to decide on their own whether they want to volunteer, they say. Some studies have also suggested that the regulations reduce students' motivation to volunteer in later life.

However, other studies show that students only lose interest if they are given boring tasks like tidying places or sorting papers during their first service. The kids who have close contact with other people and feel that their work is making a difference to them are more likely to continue to participate in service as adults. So students can actually profit from mandatory community service, but they need to do really meaningful activities.

b) Write an article in German for your school newspaper or website. Inform the other students about community service requirements in the US and discuss whether similar regulations should be introduced in German schools.

9 REVISION Tips for your job search
(Gerund or infinitive) → SB (p. 80) • GAP 13.1 (p. 71)

Complete the sentences with the verbs in brackets. Decide whether you have to use a gerund or a *to*-infinitive.

1 Can you imagine *looking for* (look for) a part-time job that would help you *to earn* (earn) some extra pocket money?

2 If you don't know what kind of job you would be good at, think about what tasks and activities you enjoy ______ (do).

3 Ask yourself if you would prefer ______ (work) indoors or outdoors.

4 Make a list of companies that might be fun ______ (work for).

5 Remember ______ (write) a simple CV.

6 You could consider ______ (apply) in person and plan ______ (go) to all the places on your list.

7 When you talk to a business owner or manager, don't forget ______ (keep) eye contact and try ______ (be) confident.

8 If it is not important to you to earn money, you could also volunteer ______ (tutor) kids that have problems at school and need to practise ______ (read) or arithmetic[5].

[1]regulation [ˌregjəˈleɪʃn] *Regelung, Bestimmung* [2]graduate [ˈɡrædjueɪt] *die Abschlussprüfung bestehen* [3]vary [ˈveəri] variieren [4]mandatory [ˈmændətri] *obligatorisch* [5]arithmetic [əˈrɪθmətɪk] *Rechnen*

10 Finding a student job (Infinitive constructions) ➜ SB (p. 80) • GAP 13 (p. 71)

a) Rewrite these sentences using a *to*-infinitive. First underline the part in the sentence that you have to change.

1 Michelle was the first person in our class who found a student job.

Michelle was the first person in our class to find a student job.

2 Diego was the only one who got over $7 per hour.

____

3 Babysitting and dogsitting are among the easiest jobs that you can do.

____

4 Is there anyone I can ask for help with finding part-time work?

____

5 Social media platforms are often the best places where you can look for adverts.

____

6 For teenagers living in villages there is often nothing that they can do to earn money.

____

b) Write these sentences in English using a *to*-infinitive.

1 Jeremy war gestern der Letzte, der mit seinen Aufgaben fertig war.

____

2 Das Einkaufszentrum in der Baker Street ist momentan der beste Ort, der Jobs für Teenager anbietet.

____

11 Which verb fits? (Infinitive constructions) ➜ SB (p. 80) • GAP 13 (p. 71)

Complete the sentences. Choose verbs from the box that fit the context. Use the *to*-infinitive.

allow · apply · ask · call · do · *create* · look for · make · speak · study · use · work · write

1 When did you make the decision *to create* an account on *Instagraph?*

2 Do you need your parents' permission ______________ when you are a minor?

3 Student job fairs provide good opportunities ______________ work.

4 What is the best format ______________ for a CV in the UK?

5 And what are some good questions for applicants ______________ in an interview?

6 Today is your last chance ______________ for summer camp jobs in Colorado Springs.

12 More spelling practice ➔ SB (p. 81)

a) 17 Listen and write down the words.

accent,

b) Check your spelling. Use the dictionary on pp. 246–285 in your student's book.

c) Sort the words from a) into the lists. (There are more words with different spellings in English and German.)

same spelling as in German	different spelling	difference in the German word	different spelling	difference in the German word
	accent	*Akzent*		

13 Tricky words (Words that sound the same) ➔ SB (p. 81)

a) Look up the word for the fruit in the photo and its pronunciation. Then explain the photo.

b) 18 Listen and complete the sentences.

1 I *rode* ______ my bike along an empty ______ in the countryside.

2 John ______ a ball ______ the neighbours' living room window.

3 Let's ______ at the market hall and buy some good ______ for our dinner party.

4 ______ is my new shirt? I'd like to ______ it to the party tonight.

5 We need to know ______ it's going to rain later. Have you heard the ______ report?

6 Millie and Fred are our best friends. ______ flat is over ______, in the red house.

7 Students easily get ______ when they have to copy long texts from the ______.

8 Our team ______ the volleyball competitions and now we're number ______ in the local league!

c) For each of these words, there is another one that sounds the same but is spelled differently. Write it down.

male – ______ sun – ______ minor – ______ ate – ______

would – ______ bean – ______ our – ______ knight – ______

14 An appointment → SB (p. 81)

a) 19 Aurelio Calascione has applied for a summer job at a water park in Colorado. Listen to the phone call. What is Aurelio's reason for calling the park? Circle A, B or C.

A to ask for an appointment B to make an appointment C to change his appointment

b) Read the questions. Then listen again and take notes.

1 Who does Aurelio want to speak to and why?

2 Who is Josie and how does she help Aurelio?

3 Why does Josie ask Aurelio to spell his last name?

4 When is Aurelio's interview?

5 What else does Aurelio ask Josie?

c) 20 Imagine you are Aurelio. Listen to Josie again and answer her questions in the pauses. Give answers similar to Aurelio's, but use your own words.

15 What résumés/CVs should look like → SB (p. 82)

a) Which elements are not necessary in a résumé/CV? Write X in the boxes.

- ◯ your hobbies and interests
- ◯ a personal statement
- ◯ your qualifications/skills
- ◯ your date of birth
- ◯ comments about former jobs
- ◯ your work experience
- ◯ your email address
- ◯ your photo
- ◯ your education
- ◯ your name
- ◯ the time when you are available
- ◯ your address

b) Now number the information that you should give about yourself in the right order.

c) High school student Lucy is looking for a part-time job and answers an advert from an online photo printing service that is located in her hometown. She is a member of her high school's photography club and has taken part in several photography workshops organized by professionals.

Look at Lucy's draft of the personal statement in her résumé and compare it with Jason's personal statement on p. 82 of your student's book. What do you notice?

Easy-going 17-year-old high school student is looking for a fun part-time job. I've taken lots of awesome pics in the past few years and now I'm aiming for a career in photography. That's why I want to improve my skills on the side. I have an eye for style and a great sense of humour. Even though I'm not the best student, I learn really fast if I'm interested in something. I like being around other people and can hold a conversation about anything.

d) ● Rewrite Lucy's personal statement in your exercise book. You can make up some pieces of information.

16 Writing a résumé ➜ SB (p. 82)

American kids have long summer holidays. A lot of them spend some time at a summer camp. These camps offer all kinds of different physical and cultural activities which allow children to learn new skills in a safe environment. Teenagers and young adults can work there as counselors. Each of them is responsible for a small group.

a) 16-year-old Allison wants to apply for a job as a camp counselor. Read the job profile and write notes about the different requirements in the list below.

CAMP COUNSELOR JOB DESCRIPTION

To succeed as a camp counselor, you should be cheerful, confident, reliable and responsible. You should also be well-organized and have strong leadership skills.

Further requirements

- High school diploma, or enrolment in school[1]
- Experience working in camps or with children
- Physical ability to take part in different activities, such as running, climbing, swimming, lifting and carrying children
- Excellent communication skills

Duties

- Living with young campers and ensuring[2] they are safe at all times
- Planning outdoor activities or sports for groups of campers and creating daily or weekly schedules for them
- Leading free-time and educational activities, such as hiking or crafting[3]
- Setting up camping equipment and ensuring that it is used correctly
- Keeping discipline within the groups
- Performing first aid or taking care of injuries if necessary

character traits: ______________________________

qualifications/skills: ______________________________

____

work experience: ______________________________

b) Use the information about Allison to write her résumé in the correct format. Look at p. 82 of your student's book for help.

Address: 3822 Glenwood Road; Boulder, CO 80304
Email: alliturner0404@jmail.com

Allison Turner is 16 years old and in grade 10 at Boulder High School. She has attended this school for three years. Before that she lived in Denver where she went to Morey Middle School. She has a current[4] GPA of 3.75. Her favorite subjects are sports, Spanish and math.
Since starting high school, Allison has been a cheerleader. Her cheerleading group trains twice a week. Last year Allison received a school award for best team player.
She has babysat two families' children (aged 2–6) on a regular basis for two years. The children's parents like her because she is very friendly and reliable. Since last summer Allison has also been a volunteer with a local charity group where she tutors immigrant children from South America in English and math on Friday afternoons. She really enjoys this job. The organizers of the charity group are pleased with her work because she is patient with the kids and able to motivate them.
In her free time, Allison likes trampolining, skiing, listening to music and reading graphic novels.

[1] enrolment [ɪnˈrəʊlmənt] in school *Schulbesuch* [2] ensure [ɪnˈʃɔː] *sicherstellen* [3] crafting [ˈkrɑːftɪŋ] *Werken, Basteln* [4] current [kʌrnt] *derzeitig*

17 Allison's letter of application ➔ SB (p. 85) • SMC 6 (p. 78), Wordbank 6

Write a letter of application for Allison. Use the job description and the information about Allison on p. 42. You can also look at p. 85 of your student's book for help.

You need this additional information:

- Address: Mr Miguel Rodriguez, Camp-o-Fun, PO Box 356, Pine Brook Hill, CO 80304
- Allison found the Camp-o-Fun job advert on the Internet (campjobs.org). They are looking for an enthusiastic counselor who is able to lead one of the sports activities.
- Allison looked at the camp's website and really liked the way it was presented.
- Allison would like to work at the camp throughout June and July.
- She has letters of reference from the two families she babysits for and from the charity group where she has been tutoring immigrant children.

Your address

Address

Date

Heading

Dear …

Paragraph 1: Say where you saw the job advert and why you are applying.
Paragraph 2: Describe your qualifications.

Conclusion

Finish

Type the letter of application on a computer.

Compare your letters and give each other feedback.

18 SPEAKING COURSE Giving good answers in a job interview ➔ SB (p. 86)

a) Allison has been invited to a job interview at Camp-o-Fun by the site director, Mr Rodriguez. Here are some of the questions he asks her. Write good answers that Allison could give in your exercise book.

1 Tell me about yourself.
2 Why are you applying for a job with Camp-o-Fun?
3 How would you describe a good camp counselor?
4 Why should we choose you for the job?
5 What are your strengths and weaknesses?
6 You have some experience working with children, but you haven't worked at a camp so far. Being a counselor is a lot of fun, but it is also quite stressful. What makes you think that you will be able to do the job?
7 You love sports and you can probably work very well with children who are just like you. But what about kids who aren't very athletic[1]? How would you try to include and motivate them?
8 I noticed that you didn't mention a first aid qualification in your résumé. When doing activities, young campers sometimes have accidents or hurt themselves. Are you able to perform first aid and take care of injuries?
9 How would you deal with a conflict between campers?

b) Practise the questions and answers.

c) Now act out the whole interview. Greet[2] each other politely at the beginning and say goodbye at the end.

d) Work with another partner. Swap roles.

[1]athletic [æθ'letɪk] *sportlich* [2]greet [gri:t] *begrüßen*

1 WORDS Describing character

a) Fill in the missing adjectives.

1 A person who shows a lot of excitement and interest in something is ______________.

2 Someone who tries very hard to win or be better than others is ______________.

3 ______________ is the opposite of lazy.

4 Someone who is ______________ tries to avoid danger and mistakes and does not take any risks.

5 Even if you are nervous in an interview, you should try to appear ______________.

6 A ______________ person is upset when someone they love is interested in another person.

b) Add prefixes to these adjectives to make the opposites.

1 responsible – ______________
2 honest – ______________
3 tolerant – ______________
4 polite – ______________
5 practical – ______________
6 emotional – ______________
7 reliable – ______________
8 regular – ______________
9 respectful – ______________

2 Which tense? (Personal passive: simple past and present perfect)

Complete the sentences with the verbs in brackets. Decide whether you have to use the simple past or the present perfect form of the personal passive.

1 Ava ______________ (send) a heart of roses last weekend, but she still doesn't know who it was from.

2 The Jacksons are trying to sell their house and ______________ (just offer) a really good price for it.

3 Luckily ______________ (not ask) any difficult questions in the history exam.

4 Logan and Wyatt ______________ (give) new mountain bikes for Christmas.

5 We want to move, but none of the apartments that we ______________ (show) so far were big enough.

6 Riley ______________ (promise) a new TV set if she passes her exams successfully.

3 How to write a letter of application

Complete the text with verbs and phrases that fit the context.

Here are some tips for letters of application. Write your ______________ at the top on the ______________. If you don't know any names, begin with ______________. If you know a name, begin with ______________. You shouldn't use ______________ forms such as *I'm* or informal language, like *great*. Write a ______________ after the main body in which you thank the person, company or organization for considering your application. Finish your letter with "Yours faithfully" or ______________.

majestic	low	rugged	bare
impressive	high	jagged	snowy
spectacular	tall		snow-covered
	towering		tree-covered
	steep		rocky

TIP: When you use more than one adjective before a noun, **comment adjectives** (e.g. beautiful, unusual) and **size adjectives** (e.g. huge, tall) usually come first and second. Other adjectives follow.
As a guideline, follow the sequence of the columns in the tables on this and the following page.
It is usually better style to use just two, or at most three, adjectives, e.g. *towering rocky mountains.*

	beautiful	large	colourful	tropical
	interesting	small	exotic	land
a/an	rare	tall	predatory	sea
	unique	short	wild	

	cute	large	tame	marine
	endangered	huge	dangerous	furry
a/an	extraordinary	small	poisonous	forest
	rare	tiny	deadly	
	unusual		wild	

	amazing	large	ancient	dense
	remarkable	colossal	pristine	green
a/an	spectacular	endless	untouched	lush
	wonderful	vast		tropical

ancient ['eɪnʃənt] *(ur)alt* **at most** *höchstens* **bare** *kahl* **colossal** [kə'lɒsl] *riesig* **dense** *dicht* **endangered** *gefährdet; vom Aussterben bedroht* **extraordinary** [ɪk'strɔːdnri] *außergewöhnlich, ungewöhnlich* **furry** ['fɜːri] *pelzig* **impressive** *beeindruckend* **jagged** ['dʒægɪd] *zerklüftet* **low** *niedrig* **lush** *üppig* **majestic** [mə'dʒestɪk] *majestätisch, mächtig* **predatory** ['predətri] *Raub-* **pristine** ['prɪstiːn] *ursprünglich, unberührt* **rare** *selten* **remarkable** *erstaunlich, bemerkenswert* **rugged** ['rʌgɪd] *rau, schroff* **sequence** ['siːkwəns] *Abfolge, Reihenfolge* **spectacular** [spek'tækjələ] *spektakulär* **tame** *zahm* **towering** *hoch aufragend* **unique** [ju'niːk] *einzigartig* **untouched** *unberührt*

Fotos: **Fotolia** (koala: Mark Galer; forest: AustralianCamera); **Shutterstock** (bird: Hugh Lansdown; mountains: Kayumov Ruslan) a/an

beautiful	long	narrow	shallow	straight
charming	large	wide	deep	winding
	short		rough	slow-moving
			gentle	fast-moving

a/an

attractive	little	wide	shallow	freshwater
lovely	large		deep	saltwater
delightful	huge			
	immense			

a/an

beautiful	long	straight	unspoilt	rocky
dramatic	extensive	curving	untouched	rugged
striking	steep			wild
stunning				

a/an

lovely	long	secluded	unspoilt	sandy
incredible	endless	lonely	pristine	golden
breathtaking	extensive		deserted	rocky
			empty	

Make phrases with each of the nouns on page I and on this page. Use two or three adjectives.

1 majestic snow-covered mountains

2 ____________

3 ____________

4. ____________

5 ____________

6 ____________

7 ____________

8 ____________

breathtaking *atemberaubend* **charming** *bezaubernd* **curving** *gekrümmt* **delightful** *entzückend, herrlich* **deserted** [dɪˈzɜːtɪd] *menschenleer, einsam* **extensive** [ɪkˈstensɪv] *ausgedehnt, weitläufig* **gentle** *sanft, sacht* **immense** *enorm* **rough** [rʌf] *rau, uneben, unwirtlich* **secluded** [sɪˈkluːdɪd] *abgeschieden, einsam* **striking** *auffallend, beeindruckend* **unspoilt** [ˌʌnˈspɔɪlt] *unberührt, unverbaut* **winding** [ˈwaɪndɪŋ] *gewunden, kurvenreich*

 Fotos: **Fotolia** (beach: Rafael Ben-Ari/Chameleons Eye; coastline: jovannig; lake: norinori303); **Shutterstock** (river: AustralianCamera)

1 Useful language for online communication

Talking about apps

You can install your apps on different devices.
Could you tell me your Wi-Fi password?
The privacy setting is set to 'Public'.
Her status says she's online/offline at the moment.
The photo has got a lot of likes.
My profile picture/pic doesn't show my face.
You can download free message tones from the internet.
I've turned on read receipts for all my apps.

Talking about technical problems

The internet connection is poor/slow.
Our connection dropped./We got cut off.
We don't have Wi-Fi here.
Your image/video is frozen.
Your image/video is blurry/pixelated.
My app crashed.
I can't see you. Please turn on your camera.
I can't hear you. You need to unmute your microphone.

2 Using digital media

You can …

choose an internet service provider.
join a social network.
spend time on social media sites.
share pictures, videos and stories with your friends.
read or write blogs.
watch vlogs on video portals.
sign up for an account with a streaming service.
connect a games console to a PC monitor.
use fitness tracker apps to view your workouts.

3 How to stay safe online

You should …

always choose strong passwords.
use different passwords for different apps.
read the privacy policies before you install apps.
check the security settings of your apps.
tell your parents if a stranger contacts you online.
report upsetting content.
ask your friends for permission if you want to post photos of them.

You shouldn't …

leave your computer open when you take a break.
use your real name in online games.
share any personal data.
fill out forms without your parents' permission.
download music or videos illegally.
click on internet links in emails from strangers.
accept friend requests or group invitations from anonymous users.

4 Collocations

change	a password
do	a search
download	apps, files, pictures, videos
edit	files, photos, videos
mute/unmute	a laptop, a microphone
post	a photo, a smiley
receive	a call, a post
scroll through	a chat, a website
take down	a photo, a post
upload	a file, a photo

anonymous [ə'nɒnɪməs] *anonym* **blurry** ['blɜːri] *undeutlich, verschwommen* **device** [dɪ'vaɪs] *Gerät* **form** *Formular* **install** [ɪn'stɔːl] *installieren* **join** *etwas beitreten* **pixelated** ['pɪksəleɪtɪd] *unscharf* **read receipt** ['riːd rɪsiːt] *Lesebestätigung* **sign up for** *sich anmelden bei* **streaming service** *Streamingdienst* **video portal** *Videoportal* **Wi-Fi** ['waɪfaɪ] *WLAN*

Fotos: **Shutterstock** (digital devices: sdecoret; smart phones: Damiano Buffo)

1 Useful adjectives

affectionate
[ə'fekʃnət]
liebevoll

alarmed
[ə'lɑːmd]
beunruhigt

amused
[ə'mjuːzd]
vergnügt, belustigt

astonished
[ə'stɒnɪʃt]
erstaunt

blissful
['blɪsfl]
glückselig

concerned
[kən'sɜːnd]
betroffen

confident
['kɒnfɪdənt]
(selbst)sicher

confused
[kən'fjuːzd]
verwirrt, irritiert

content
[kən'tent]
zufrieden

delighted
[dɪ'laɪtɪd]
erfreut

depressed
[dɪ'prest]
deprimiert

disgusted
[dɪs'gʌstɪd]
angewidert

embarrassed
[ɪm'bærəst]
verlegen

exhausted
[ɪg'zɔːstɪd]
erschöpft

flattered
['flætəd]
geschmeichelt

frustrated
[frʌ'streɪtɪd]
frustriert

furious
['fjʊəriəs]
wütend

gleeful
['gliːfl]
schadenfroh

hysterical
[hɪ'sterɪkl]
ausgelassen heiter

indifferent
[ɪn'dɪfrənt]
gleichgültig

irritated
['ɪrɪteɪtɪd]
genervt

naughty
['nɔːti]
frech, unartig

upset
[ʌp'set]
bestürzt, traurig

vulnerable
['vʌlnərəbl]
verletzlich

worried
['wʌrid]
besorgt

2 Idiomatic expressions

Positive feelings

to be head over heels in love
Hals über Kopf verliebt sein
to be on top of the world
überglücklich sein
to be on the same wavelength
auf der gleichen Wellenlänge sein
to look on the bright side
die Dinge positiv sehen
to walk on air
auf Wolken schweben, im siebten Himmel sein

Negative feelings

to be beside yourself (with anger, worry, …)
neben sich stehen (vor Wut, Sorge …)
to be bored to tears
sich zu Tode langweilen
to be down in the dumps
sich niedergeschlagen fühlen
to go up the wall
die Wände hochgehen
to have a chip on one's shoulder
in reizbarer Stimmung sein

 Illustrationen: Shutterstock (pingebat)

1 Different ways of presenting statistics

a bar chart

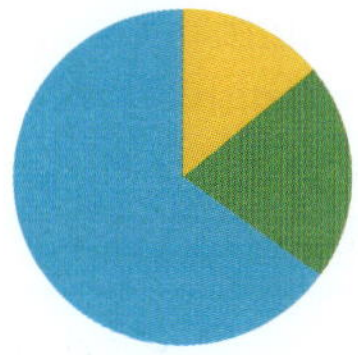

a pie chart

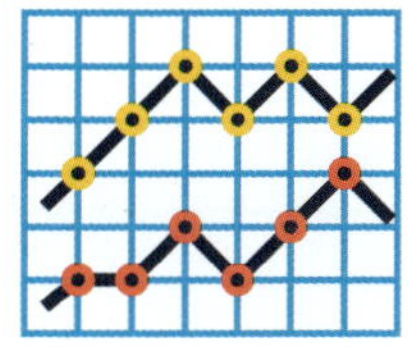

a line graph

age group	average amount of pocket money
8–10	£6.20
11–13	£9.30
14–16	£12.50

a table

2 Talking about statistics

Class survey: How much time do you spend on your mobile every day?

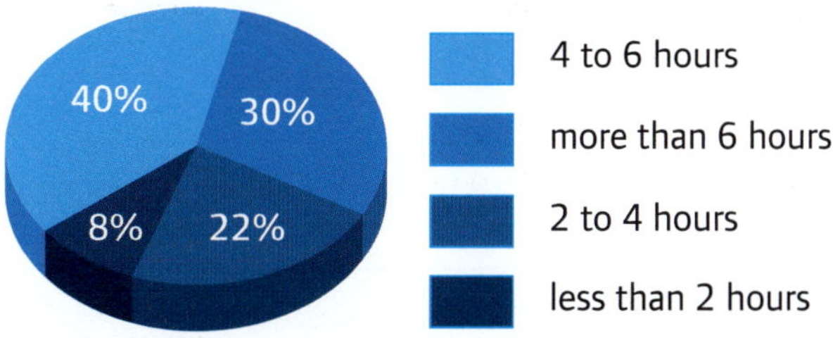

What percentage of people in your class spend more than six hours on their mobiles every day?

30 per cent.

How many citizens of Happyville were born in Mexico?

More than 27,000.

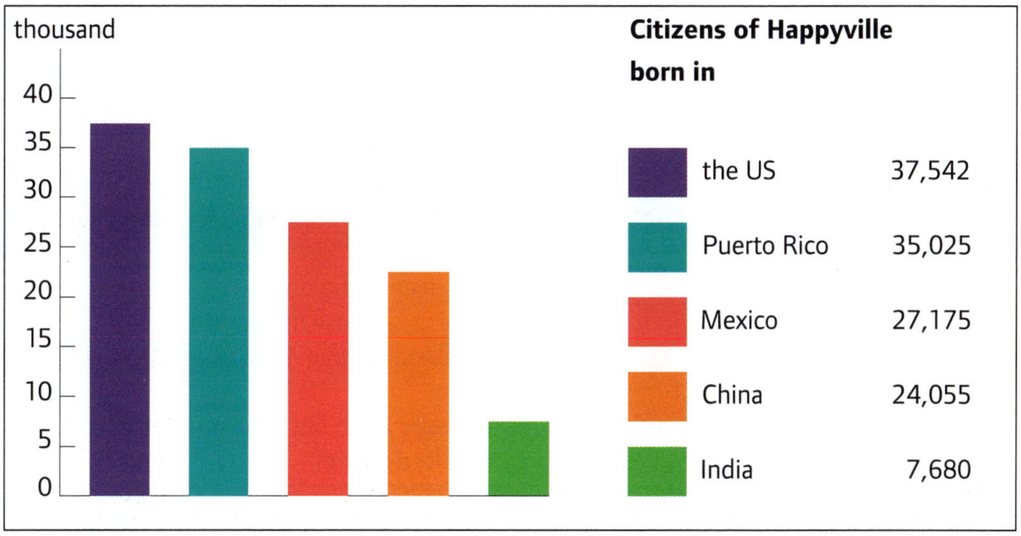

Useful language

The bar chart/pie chart/line graph/table is about …
The pie chart shows what percentage of students/how many students use …
The bar chart gives us information about the number/how many …
Only 8 per cent of students …
Five times as many students …
If you compare the number of citizens born in …
More than 35,000 people …
Fewer than 8,000 people …

Write ten or more sentences about the two charts in your exercise book.

Grafiken: **Shutterstock** (bar chart, pie chart above, line graph: A Aleksii; pie chart below: aiconsmith)

Wordbank 6: Letter of application

How to start

If you don't know who you are writing to
Dear Sir
Dear Madam
Dear Sir/Madam

If you know who you are writing to
Dear Mr Smith
Dear Mrs Smith
Dear Ms Smith

The first sentence

I am writing to apply for …
I wish to apply for the position/post of … which you advertised in … on …
I read your advertisement for a … in … with great interest.
I refer to your advertisement in … dated …
I would like to apply for the internship …
I am writing about your internship program which was advertised in …
As discussed on the phone today, I am sending you my personal documentation.
Having completed my training as a/an …, I am now looking for a post/a job/a career in …

Your education/qualifications

I am currently attending … School and I am in Year/Grade …
I am currently a student/employed at …
I will graduate this year with a high school diploma/…
I graduated from … in …
I have completed the following courses: …
I hold a certificate/degree in …
I have been working as a/an …

Giving information about yourself

I am particularly interested in this job because …
I would like to work for you in order to …
My strengths are …
Currently I am working for … and my responsibilities include …
During … I did an internship in …/at …/abroad.
During my time as …, I improved my knowledge of …
Even under pressure I can maintain high standards.
In addition to my responsibilities as …, I developed … skills.

What skills you have acquired

I have experience of …
As my references show, …
As you can see from my CV/résumé, I have a strong interest in …
I feel I have the necessary qualities for this job because …
I am a motivated student/professional with a variety of skills and experience.
I would be well suited to the job/position because …
I have a working knowledge of …
During … I have taken a great interest in working (together) with …
This job would give me the opportunity to extend my knowledge of … /to use my IT skills.
I wish to work abroad and make use of my knowledge of languages.
My native language is …, but I can also speak …
I am an experienced user of …

How to finish

I can give you the following names as references: …
I have attached my CV/résumé and the address of … They will be pleased to send you a letter of reference./He/She has agreed to be my referee.
I am available for an interview/a video interview at any time.
Thank you for considering my application.
I would be delighted to be invited to an interview.
I look forward to meeting you/hearing from you (soon).
I see new tasks/this position as a welcome challenge, which I look forward to.

If you don't know who you are writing to
Yours faithfully,

If you know who you are writing to
Yours sincerely,

acquire [ə'kwaɪə] *erwerben* **delight** [dɪ'laɪt] *erfreuen* **Yours faithfully** ['feɪθfəli] *Mit freundlichen Grüßen* **graduate** ['grædʒueɪt] *einen (Schul-) Abschluss machen* **particularly** [pə'tɪkjələli] *besonders* **suited** [suːtɪd] *geeignet*

Describing a language

a **first**/a **native**/an **indigenous** language
a **mother**/a **native** tongue
a **foreign**/a **non-native**/an **unfamiliar** language
a **second**/an **additional**/an **official** language
a **common**/a **shared** language
a **world**/a **global**/a **universal**/an **international** language

Complete sentence 1 and write a second sentence using words from the box above.

1 My native language is ______________ and I speak ____________ as a/an ______________ language.

2 ____

Talking about communication

A language is **a medium/a means/a tool** of communication.
(to) speak English/French/… **fluently/adequately/poorly**
(to) need an **interpreter/a translator/…**
(to) communicate **across languages/across national borders/in a globalized world**
(to) **be fluent in/communicate through/correspond through/negotiate through** English/French/…

Complete these sentences using words or phrases from the two boxes above.

1 If you are fluent in ____

2 If you want to communicate across ______________________________________

How languages are used

English **French** **Latin** …	is/was **used** has been/was **introduced** has been/was **adopted**	for in	**international/official/written** communication. international **correspondence/negotiations**.
		by	**the church/the government/the upper class.** **churchmen/civil servants/diplomats.** **scholars/scientists/explorers.**
	is has become was became	**the language of**	**advertising/business/commerce/trade.** **administration/government/diplomacy.** **aviation/air traffic control/shipping.** **education/research/science/technology/ scholarship/religion.**

Write two sentences using the words in brackets and words or phrases from the box above.

1 (the Middle Ages, Latin) ____

2 (English, trade and diplomacy) ____

additional [ə'dɪʃənl] *zusätzliche(r, s)* **adequately** ['ædɪkwətli] *ausreichend* **administration** [əd,mɪnɪ'streɪʃn] *Verwaltung* **adopt** *übernehmen, annehmen* **air traffic control** *Flugsicherung* **civil servant** *Beamte(r)* **commerce** ['kɒmɜːs] *Handel* **correspond** [,kɒrə'spɒnd] *korrespondieren* **correspondence** *Korrespondenz, Briefwechsel* **fluent** ['fluːənt] *fließend* **interpreter** [ɪn'tɜːprɪtə] *Dolmetscher/in* **means** *Mittel* **medium** *Medium, Mittel* **mother tongue/native tongue** [tʌŋ] *Muttersprache* **negotiate** [nɪ'gəʊʃieɪt] *verhandeln* **negotiation** [nɪ,gəʊʃi'eɪʃn] *Verhandlung* **poorly** *schlecht* **scholarship** *Wissenschaft* **shipping** *Schifffahrt* **the Middle Ages** *das Mittelalter* **universal** [,juːnɪ'vɜːsl] *universell* **upper class** *Oberschicht*

Starting a presentation
Good morning/afternoon everybody. It's nice to see you all today.
I'm/We're going to talk about …
My/Our topic today is …
I've divided my talk into … parts. Firstly, I'll talk about … Then, we'll look at … I'll finish by talking about …
Let's start with …

Introducing new parts and ideas
My first/next/last point is …
Let's first turn to …
Now let's look at …
I'd like to move on to …
Another important aspect is …
Another idea/issue I'd like to tell you about is …
In addition to this, …
This brings me/us to the next point …

Clarifying
In other words, …
That means …
That is to say …
What I'm saying is …
What I mean by … is …
To put that another way, …
Let me rephrase that.
Let me explain that again.

Referring to media and visuals
My poster shows …
Look at this photo. It shows …
Please look at/have a look at …
As you can see on this slide, …
I'd now like to draw your attention to …
To illustrate this, let's look more closely at …
If you compare these diagrams/pictures …, you will certainly notice that …

Recapping ideas
As I said/mentioned/explained earlier, …
As I've already explained, …
Let me come back to what I talked about before.
Let's go back to what we discussed earlier.
As I pointed out in the first section, …
I'd now like to go back to a point I mentioned at the beginning.
You will remember what I said about …

Involving the audience
Do you see what I mean?
Don't you agree?
What do you think?
You all certainly know …
Did you know that …?
You've probably seen this before.
You may have heard that …
Does anyone have an idea why …?

Summing up and closing your talk
To summarise, …
So, my main points have been …
Let me remind you of some of the topics we've covered.
That brings us to the end of my talk. I'd like to thank you all for your attention.
Do you have any questions?
Feel free to ask questions now.

Giving positive feedback on a presentation
You spoke loudly and clearly.
You made eye contact with the audience.
Your presentation was easy to follow.
Your presentation had a clear structure.
You gave interesting information.
I learned a lot from your presentation.
I liked how you …
You chose really good/excellent/… visuals.

Giving tips on how to improve presentations
Next time you could try to …
In your next presentation you might …
Perhaps you could …
It might be helpful to …
In the future you might consider …
It always helps me to … Maybe you could also try to do it like that.
I think you could easily avoid … if you …

clarify ['klærɪfaɪ] *etwas klarstellen* **involve** [ɪn'vɒlv] *hier: einbeziehen* **recap** ['riːkæp] *kurz zusammenfassen* **visuals** ['vɪʒuəlz] *Bildmaterial*

 Foto: Shutterstock (Syda Productions)

4 Applying for a summer job

a) Read the job advert.

Lifeguard
Oasis Pools; 6700 Del Rey Rd; Las Cruces, NM 84056

Wage: $13 an hour **Job type:** part-time **Age:** 16+
Working hours: 10 to 35 per week, Monday through Sunday

Are you looking for a fun job in the sun? Then come join us as a lifeguard this summer!

Required qualifications and skills

- Strong swimming skills
- Ability to sit or stand for long periods at a time
- Polite and patient behaviour as well as good communication skills
- Flexibility regarding scheduling of working hours
- No work experience required; paid training in first aid, CPR[1] and basic water rescue will be provided

Duties and responsibilities

- Carefully observing[2] the pool area at all times
- Disciplining people who break the pool safety rules
- Responding quickly to any emergency situation
- Treating minor injuries with basic first aid
- Performing daily routine chores to ensure the tidy appearance of the pool

b) Write a letter of application for 16-year-old Mateo. Include this information:

- Mateo Garcia's address: 6717 Burroughs Drive; Las Cruces, NM 80007; email: matgarcia@zmail.com
- Mateo saw the advert on summerjobs.us.
- He has been a member of his high school's swim team for four years. He can swim 50 yards in four foot deep water and pick up a 10-pound brick from the bottom of the pool.
- He has done small jobs for elderly people, doing the shopping for them and mowing[3] their lawns.
- He would like to work at Oasis Pools from mid-June through August. He has a letter of reference from his swim coach, Mr Norman Hart.

Check: Writing

a) Vergleiche deine Antworten mit den Lösungen auf Seite 88 in diesem Workbook.
b) Schätze deine Antworten mit einem grünen oder roten Gesicht ein.

	☺	☹	
1 WORDS Describing character Kanntest du die Bedeutung verschiedener Adjektive?	○	○	→ 1
3 How to write a letter of application Hast du gewusst, wie man einen formellen Brief schreibt?	○	○	→ 2
4 Applying for a summer job 1 Hast du in 4b) den richtigen Aufbau einer Bewerbung beachtet?	○	○	→ 3
2 Hast du in 4b) passende Formulierungen gewählt und die Bewerbung im korrekten Format geschrieben?	○	○	→ 4

c) Wenn du dich mit rot eingeschätzt hast, schau dir die rechte Spalte an. Die Nummern führen dich zu den passenden Übungen im Skills Training (S. 46-47). Dort kannst du gezielt das Schreiben trainieren.

[1] CPR *Herz-Lungen-Wiederbelebung* [2] observe [əbˈzɜːv] *beobachten* [3] mow [məʊ] *mähen*

1 Using suitable adjectives

TIP: When describing yourself, it is often good to use adverbs like *quite, not very, (not) usually, fairly* or *mostly* before the adjectives. Example: I'm **quite hard-working and usually competitive**.

To avoid sounding arrogant, you can begin with phrases like *My friends/people say …* *I always try to be …*
Example: **People say** I'm polite and **I always try to be** helpful.

a) Choose positive and negative adjectives to describe a person's character from the box. Some adjectives don't fit into either list.

open · creative · dishonest · happy · easy-going · friendly · hard-working · nervous · helpful · impatient · intolerant · young · lazy · mean · practical · relaxed · responsible · tired · rude · cruel · unkind · self-confident · desperate · excited · untidy

positive adjectives:

____

____

negative adjectives:

____

____

b) Describe your own character. Your text should be serious and honest and it should not sound arrogant. You can use adjectives from a) and/or other adjectives. Consider the tip too.

____

____

____

2 Get it right

These parts of a letter of application aren't perfect. Make the necessary changes in style, vocabulary and content.

23. Oct., 2022 ______________________________

Your ad ______________________________

Hello, Mrs Peters, ______________________________

I'm writing to you about the hotel job. ______________________________

____

I'm a quick learner and it's easy for me to talk to people. ______________________________

____

Please let me know as soon as possible if you're going to give me the job. ______________________________

____

Bye, yours, Melanie Ann Foster ______________________________

3 An internship at a zoo ➔ *SMC 6 (p. 78)*

a) 17-year-old Jayden is applying for an animal care internship at Denver Zoo. Number the parts of his letter of application in the right order.

☐ Dear Ms Bernstein,

☐ Jayden Breckenridge
4871 E 91st Avenue
Denver, CO 80194
Email: jayden0811@abl.com

☐ 2nd May 20..

☐ Yours sincerely,
Jayden Breckenridge

☐ **Your advert**

☐ Denver Zoo
Ms Sarah Bernstein
2900 E 23rd Avenue
Denver, CO 80205

☐ Last summer I stayed with my aunt and uncle in Norfolk and took part in the Virginia Zoo's Conservation Youth Team (CYT) program for seven weeks. The program is offered to high school volunteers. I learned a lot about animals and conservation during my stay there and was able to develop some important skills.

☐ I am writing to apply for the animal care internship, as advertised on your website. I am very interested in the position because I would like to become a vet.

☐ Thank you for considering my application. I look forward to hearing from you.

b) Mark the parts that have to be on the right.

4 A letter of application ➔ *SMC 6 (p. 78), Wordbank 6*

In the US, students can go to summer school to improve their performance at school or to progress more quickly.

Read the job advert for a summer school student helper and write a letter of application for an American teenager who is the right person for the job. Make up information about him or her.

Summer School Student Helper
Austin Independent School District
4000 S. I-H 35 Frontage Rd., Austin, TX 78704

Salary: $10 an hour **Job type:** temporary **Age:** 16+
Working hours: 27.5 hours per week, Monday through Friday, 9:30 a.m.–3:00 p.m.

Helpers will assist the Summer School staff during the programs and perform some simple office tasks as needed.

Required qualifications and skills
- High School diploma
- Professional and helpful attitude when dealing with staff, students and parents
- Strong leadership and decision-making skills
- Excellent telephone and oral[1] communication skills
- General office skills

Duties and responsibilities
- Assist teachers in preparing materials and activities
- Help individual students or small groups with exercises assigned by the teachers
- Assist in supervising[2] students inside and outside the classroom
- Answer phone calls and write formal notes
- Ensure the safety of the classroom and playground

[1] oral ['ɔːrəl] *mündlich* [2] *supervise* ['suːpəvaiz] *beaufsichtigen*

New Zealand

1 An amazing country ➜ SB (pp. 90–91) • SMC 21 (p. 83)

a) 21 Listen to a podcast episode about New Zealand and answer the questions.

1 Which ocean surrounds New Zealand? ____________________

2 On which of the two main islands is Wellington located?

____

b) Listen again and tick the right answers.

1 How long did Samantha and Alex stay in New Zealand?

◯ for four weeks ◯ for five weeks ◯ for six weeks

2 How many smaller islands belong to New Zealand?

◯ about 60 ◯ about 500 ◯ about 600

3 Which is the largest city in New Zealand?

◯ Auckland ◯ Christchurch ◯ Wellington

4 How many sheep are there in New Zealand?

◯ about 30,000 ◯ about 30 million ◯ about 130 million

5 How many official languages are there in New Zealand?

◯ two ◯ three ◯ four

6 How many places have Samantha and Alex chosen for their list of tips for travellers?

◯ 12 ◯ 15 ◯ 20

2 Environmental issues ➜ SB (pp. 92–93)

○ Complete the sentences with words from pp. 92-93 of your student's book.

1 p o l l u t i o n is damage caused to nature by waste and _ _ _ _ i c _ _ _.

2 The _ _ t _ _ s _ _ _ c _ _ _ _ n of _ g r _ _ _ _ t _ _ _ causes huge problems.

3 CO_2 is a _ _ _ _ _ h _ _ _ _ _ _ _ that is one cause of global warming.

4 Using _ o _ _ _ _ _ _ _ g y is a _ _ _ m _ _ e - _ r _ _ _ d _ _ alternative to other ways of producing electric[1] power.

5 In _ _ _ _ _ i c f _ _ _ _ _ _, food is produced using natural methods.

6 S _ _ _ a i _ _ _ _ _ solutions are the only way to stop c _ _ _ _ _ _ c _ _ _ _ _.

[1] electric [ɪ'lektrɪk] *elektrisch*

3 REVISION Perhaps they will … (Predictions with *will* and *might*) ➔ SB (p. 94) • GAP 6.2 (p. 66)

a) Look at the photos. What do you think the people will do? Write two predictions for each photo. Use the phrases in the box.

I think the boy/the girl/… will/won't … · I don't think … · … will probably/probably won't … · Perhaps/Maybe … · … might (not) …

1 ____________________

2 ____________________

3 ____________________

4 ____________________

b) Compare your ideas and discuss them.

4 REVISION What's going to happen? (Predictions with the *going to*-future) ➔ SB (p. 94) • GAP 6.1 (p. 66)

Write down the people's predictions or warnings about what is going to happen or not going to happen in the following situations. You can use *I'm sure …* or *It looks like …* if it fits the situation.

1 Mila is at a football match with some friends. It's 3 to 1 for their team in the second half. Mila says to the others:

It looks like our team is going to win.

2 Ian's family's old car is broken and they need a new one soon. Ian tells a friend:

____

3 Liam's sister wants to go into town. The bus leaves in five minutes and she's still at home. Liam says to her:

____

4 Sierra has forgotten to buy her best friend a present for her birthday. Sierra thinks:

____

5 Cody has booked a three-week holiday at a summer camp near Auckland. Cody tells a classmate:

____

6 Poppy has tickets for the cinema, but her friend hasn't arrived yet. While Poppy is waiting, she thinks:

____

5 REVISION Help for Emily (Future forms: mixed) ➜ SB (p. 95) • GAP 6, 7 (pp. 66-67)

Complete the dialogue between two British students. Decide whether you can use the present progressive, the *going to*-future or the *will*-future. Use short forms.

Note: Often there are different possibilities. Look at the tips for help.

Emily: I have to prepare a presentation about the effects of climate change in New Zealand. I think I *'m going to start* (start) early next week. I have to do it on my own, so I'm sure it ____________ (be) a lot of work.

Harry: Oh, I ____________ (help) you if you like. I've just done a similar project. I ____________ (show) you my material.

Emily: Really? That's so nice of you. What about Monday after school?

Harry: I ____________ (meet up) with a couple of friends on Monday, but I've got time on Tuesday.

Emily: I ____________ (go) to the dentist at 3:30 on Tuesday, but I ____________ (be) back by 4:30. I ____________ (call) you when I get home.

Harry: Great. I ____________ (come over) then.

> **TIP 1:** *Will* and *be going to* are often used in similar ways. You have used both to make predictions (exercises 4 and 5).
>
> You also use *will*
> – to talk about facts in the future: *We will have more rooms in our new flat.*
> – if you are certain about something: *Duncan won't come to your party because he broke his foot last week.*
> – for spontaneous decisions: *It's dark. I'll take you home.*
>
> You can use *be going to* to talk about an intention or a concrete plan: *Jocelyn says she is going to eat healthier food from now on.*

> **TIP 2:** In many situations the differences between the *going to*-future and the present progressive do not matter.
>
> You can say: *Joe is travelling to Ireland in June.*
> Or: *Joe is going to travel to Ireland in June.*
>
> However, remember that the present progressive is only used to refer to the future if a date is mentioned or if it is clear from the context that you are talking about a future action.
> *Nadira is coming over tonight. We're cooking dinner together.*
>
> You can't use the present progressive to make predictions.

6 REVISION Holidays at home (Present progressive and *going to*-future) ➜ SB (p. 95) • GAP 6, 7 (pp. 66-67)

These people are going to stay at home in the summer holidays. Complete what they say about their plans. Use the present progressive or the *going to*-future.

Martha: There's a new skate park in town and I ____________ (practise) some cool tricks.

Quinn: In the first week of the holidays my cousin from Wellington ____________ (stay) with me.

Macy: My sisters and I ____________ (have) a good time on our grandparents' farm.

Fred: At the end of July my boyfriend and I ____________ (go) to a rock festival.

Willow: I ____________ (work) in a supermarket because I'm saving for a trip to New Zealand.

Manou: My birthday is on 2nd August and I ____________ (throw) a garden party.

7 I'll be walking the dogs (Future progressive) ➜ SB (p. 96) • GAP 7.1 (p. 67)

Complete the sentences with future progressive forms of the verbs in the box.

do · pass · spend · study · walk · work

1 Try to call me after 9 o'clock. Before that I *'ll be walking* the dogs.

2 Hey Charlotte. Dad says he can drive us to music school tomorrow because he ______________________.

3 Do you want me to buy anything for dinner? I ______________________ a supermarket on my way home.

4 My mum ______________________ the next few weeks with my grandparents because my grandma is ill.

5 Milo ______________________ an internship on an organic farm throughout August.

6 Roxanne hopes that in two years' time she ______________________ Agricultural Sciences at Auckland University.

8 By the end of the month ... (Future perfect simple) ➜ SB (p. 96) • GAP 6.3 (p. 66)

Use these phrases to write statements in the future perfect simple.

1 by end of month – workers on Tilly's farm – finish building new barn

By the end of the month the workers on Tilly's farm will have finished building a new barn.

2 next June – my grandparents – be married for fifty years

____

3 Layla and Ahmed – not receive our parcel – by Saturday

____

4 at end of year – Richardson family – be in new house for one year

____

9 Say it right (Future forms: mixed) ➜ SB (p. 96) • GAP 6, 7 (pp. 66-67)

Can you use different forms of the future now? Read the sentences and tick the right endings. In one case, two answers are correct.

1 As Zac keeps playing games on his mobile, ...
- he won't be finishing his assignment in time. ◯
- he won't finish his assignment in time. ◯
- he isn't finishing his assignment in time. ◯

2 From 10 to 12 tomorrow ...
- we will be performing our school musical. ◯
- we're going to perform our school musical. ◯
- we will have performed our school musical. ◯

3 Betsy is cold. Boris says,
- "I'll be getting you a blanket." ◯
- "I might get you a blanket." ◯
- "I'll get you a blanket." ◯

4 Hopefully, by this time next month ...
- Indie will have passed all her exams. ◯
- Indie will pass all her exams. ◯
- Indie will be passing all her exams. ◯

10 WORDS Social and political involvement ➜ SB (p. 97)

a) Look at these word lists. Match them with the topics in the box.

discrimination · environmental issues · political activities · state

________________: government, parliament, citizens, political parties

________________: racism, sexism, prejudice, bullying

________________: campaign, demonstration, petition, referendum

________________: pollution, climate change, intensive farming, greenhouse gases

b) Think of four or more words that go with these topics.

nature: ________________

rights: ________________

11 WORDS Collocations ➜ SB (p. 97)

a) In the box on the right you will find the nouns from exercise 2 on p. 97 of your student's book. Make another list of collocations with the verbs in the box on the left. Use a dictionary if necessary. Sometimes you can link a noun with different verbs.

be · conduct · contact · draft · experience · hold · launch · make · pass · promote · protect · stage · wave

activist · banner · civil rights · democracy · demonstration · investment · law · movement · MP · petition · referendum · racism

________________ ________________ ________________

________________ ________________ ________________

________________ ________________ ________________

________________ ________________ ________________

b) Complete the sentences with the right prepositions.

against · for · in · on · to

1 Greenpeace is an international organization that campaigns ________ environmental issues.

2 Its activists often campaign ________ companies whose business practices harm the environment.

3 Millions of young people around the world have taken part ________ the Fridays for Future demonstrations.

4 They take ________ the streets to call for action from government and industry leaders to prevent climate change.

5 Have you ever demonstrated ________ government decisions?

6 It is important to demonstrate peacefully ________ an issue.

7 Last week a group of Māori protested ________ racial discrimination in schools.

8 Some communities have started an educational initiative to take a stand ________ racial equality.

12 EXTRA BACKGROUND FILE Australia and New Zealand → SB (pp. 98–99) • SMC 12 (p. 80)

a) Look at pp. 98–99 of your student's book again and take notes about different aspects of Australia and New Zealand.

	Australia	New Zealand
size	*about 7,700,000 sq km* *almost 26 m inhabitants*	
location		
climate		
landscapes		
wildlife		

b) Quiz a partner. Take turns.

A: *Which of the two countries has a mild climate?* – B: *That's …*

B: *What's the landscape like in the west of Australia?* – A: *There are …*

Kings Canyon, Central Australia

Franz Josef Glacier, New Zealand

13 Cathedral Cove Walk ➔ SB (p. 100) • SMC 12 (p. 80)

a) ○ You are planning to go to New Zealand with your family and each person is doing some internet research. Next weekend you want to sit down together and tell each other what you have found out.

Read the information from an official website. Find the place on a map.

Cathedral Cove Walk

Located in the Hahei area of the Coromandel peninsula (North Island)

Fitness required: moderate
Distance: 2.5 km (one way)
Gradient: undulating with steps
Time: 1:30 h return

Voted as one of the 102 must-dos for Kiwis

Description

The Cathedral Cove Walk is a popular coastal trail and is excellently maintained. The main path leads you from the northern end of Hahei along the coastline, through rugged farmland and native bush. You can go the most direct way or include some scenic routes to special attractions. If you like snorkelling, Gemstone and Stingray Bays will be perfect places for you. Another short detour takes you to a viewing platform which is located at the top of a steep cliff and offers breathtaking views. At the end of the trail, you descend to the coast where a spectacular natural rock arch separates the two beaches of Cathedral Cove. Due to its golden sand and crystal clear waters, this marvellous place is one of the most photographed spots in New Zealand.

Boat Tours operate from the Whitianga Wharf and Ferry Landing. They convey fascinating information about the geology of the area and offer you the chance to see marine wildlife such as whales, dolphins, seals and penguins.

What to know before you go

Hazards
- Rapidly changing weather conditions
- Possibility of rockfall under and around the arch
- Danger of falling rocks at the northwestern end of Stingray Bay – this area is closed.

Be prepared
- Be sure to take food and water.
- Wear sturdy shoes.
- Take away all your rubbish.

Car parking

Cathedral Cove Park and Ride is available from the Hahei visitor car park. The shuttle costs $7 return per person, $4 for a child and $14 for a family (2 adults and 2 children). Parking is free all day.
The top car park on Grange Road is a pick-up and drop-off zone for the shuttle. Parking is prohibited at Grange Road from 01 October – 30 April. Limited parking is available from 1 May – 30 September at $15 for 4 hours.

b) Your family asks you these questions. Take notes in your exercise book.

1 Warum lohnt es sich, diesen Ausflug zu machen?
2 Wie lang und wie anstrengend ist der Wanderweg?
3 Kann man auch anders als zu Fuß nach Cathedral Cove gelangen? Falls ja, wäre das besser?
4 Wo befindet sich der Weg denn genau?
5 Müssen wir etwas Besonderes beachten?
6 Wie weit kommen wir mit unserem Mietwagen und wie hoch sind die Parkgebühren?

14 WORDS Going to other places ➜ *SB (p. 101)*

a) 16-year-old Ron from Bristol went to New Zealand on his own to visit his aunt's family. Complete the report about his flight with words from exercises 8 and 9 on p. 101 of your student's book.

Ron didn't book his flight to New Zealand at a ________________ because he could get a cheaper one online. At the airport, he checked in his ____________, just one large suitcase, and went on to ________________ control where an officer carefully compared his face with the photo. At ________________________, Ron had to take off his trainers and empty his pockets. He was so tired that he fell asleep while waiting at the gate and didn't hear the first ____________________________, but fortunately he woke up a few minutes later. On the plane, a ________________________ soon served the passengers a meal, so Ron felt better. As it was a twelve-hour flight, he had enough time to study his new ___________________ and read through the tour _____________ that his aunt Liza and her family had sent him. They were planning to go on several _______________ with him. Ron liked sports and hoped they would go ________________ in the mountains for several days. He was really looking forward to _____________________ different parts of New Zealand and meeting interesting new people. Even though the language was the same, it would still be a _______________ country for him.

b) Read the definitions and write down the words.

1 The money that is used in a country: ________________

2 An official document or a stamp in your passport which allows you to enter a country: ____________

3 Cream or oil that you put on your skin so it doesn't get burned by the sun: ________________

4 A place where people on holiday can put up tents or park their caravans: ________________

5 A large building at an airport where passengers arrive or leave: ________________

6 A place for people to stay, live or work: __________________________

7 A traditional way of behaving in a society: _______________

c) Circle the correct prepositions.

1 The train to Christchurch leaves **on | from** platform 8.

2 Ron stayed **with | by** his aunt in Kaikoura.

3 Being British, he didn't have to apply **for | on** a visa.

4 This is our stop. Let's get **from | off** the bus.

5 When travelling in New Zealand, you can get from the North to the South Island **by | on** ferry.

15 How life in Aotearoa has changed over time ➜ SB (p. 102)

○ Look at the text on p. 102 of your student's book again and read the statements below. Tick T for true, F for false and N for not in the text.

	T	F	N
1 The Polynesian settlers lived in tribes that didn't have the same culture and language.	○	○	○
2 The tribes lived peacefully together on the islands which they had discovered.	○	○	○
3 Aotearoa means "land of the long white cloud."	○	○	○
4 The first people to settle in New Zealand were a small group from Holland.	○	○	○
5 The extinction of native wildlfe was due to the fact that the British settlers, who first arrived in the 18th century, brought animals and plants with them.	○	○	○
6 The English version of the Treaty of Waitangi was translated into Māori in one night.	○	○	○
7 Efforts to improve the Māori's lives finally began in the early 21st century.	○	○	○
8 147 years after the Treaty of Waitangi was signed, te reo became an official language.	○	○	○

16 REVISION Explorers (Defining and non-defining relative clauses) ➜ SB (p. 104) • GAP 15.1, 15.3 (pp. 72-73)

a) Look at these sentences. Are the relative clauses in them defining or non-defining? Add commas where needed.

1 Willem Jansz and Jan Carstensz were two Dutch explorers who had travelled to Australia before Abel Tasman.

2 Tasman who worked for the Dutch East India Company discovered New Zealand and parts of Australia.

3 The Abel Tasman National Park which was named after him is a popular tourist destination.

4 Tonga and the Fiji islands were among the other places which Tasman was the first European to see.

b) Make these sentences into a sentence which includes a relative clause. Use commas where needed.

1 James Cook was a British captain. He is considered one of the greatest sailors of all time.

James Cook was a British captain who is considered one of the greatest sailors of all time.

a statue of Captain Cook in London

2 Cook went on three expeditions to the South Pacific. He had travelled to the North Atlantic before that.

____

3 A group of scientists made lists of thousands of unknown plants and animals. The scientists accompanied Cook.

____

____

4 Cook also created maps. They showed the whole coastline of New Zealand and the eastern coast of Australia.

____

____

17 REVISION Past and present (Defining relative clauses: contact clauses)

➔ SB (p. 104) • GAP 15.2 (p. 73)

a) Is the relative pronoun the subject or the object of the relative clause in these sentences? Tick the right answer.

	Relative pronoun = subject	Relative pronoun = object
1 The Māori are people **who** show great respect for life.	◯	◯
2 The old customs **that** they follow are important parts of Kiwi life.	◯	◯
3 Pressing noses is a form of greeting **which** the Māori continue to use.	◯	◯
4 Some still have traditional tattoos **which** express their cultural identity.	◯	◯

b) Decide whether you can leave out the relative pronoun in these sentences. Cross it out if possible.

1 According to legends, the first Māori came to New Zealand from a tropical island **which** they called Hawaiki.

2 They were able to make the voyage because they had built heavy canoes **that** were up to 40 metres long.

3 In their new country, they carried on the traditions **that** they had received from their ancestors.

4 After the settlers had arrived, the Māori lost much of the land **which** they had owned for centuries.

5 For a long time, the Māori experienced forms of discrimination **that** did not let them have full civil rights.

6 Pressure groups have fought for legal and social changes **which** have improved the Māori's lives.

c) Rewrite the sentences in b) as sentences with contact clauses, where possible.

____

____

____

18 The British and te reo (Relative clauses to comment)

➔ SB (p. 105) • GAP 15.4 (p. 73)

Make one sentence out of two. Make the second sentence a relative clause that refers to the first part.

1 The early settlers often needed the Māori's support. That made it necessary for them to learn te reo.

The early settlers often needed the Māori's support, which made it necessary for them to learn te reo.

2 Their children grew up with Māori peers. This helped them to learn the indigenous language easily.

____

3 By the 1860's, many British people had arrived. This led to English becoming the main language.

____

4 Speaking te reo was then often forbidden. That shows that the British did not respect Māori culture.

____

5 The Māori continued to speak te reo in their communities. That made the language survive.

____

19 ACCESS TO CULTURES Haka – an old Māori tradition ➜ SB (p. 106) • SMC 21 (p. 83)

a) 22 Listen to an interview on an internet radio show and answer the questions. Take notes in your exercise book.

The All Blacks performing a haka

1 Why have Nikau and his rugby team come to the UK?
2 What do people do when they perform a haka?
3 Why did the Māori perform the haka in the past?
4 At which private events are hakas typically performed?
5 Who can perform the haka?
6 What examples does Nikau give to show how important the haka is in New Zealand society?
7 How do young Māori feel about the haka?

b) Do you think there are any traditions that should be respected more in German culture, e.g. traditions that are important to some minorities? Why or why not? Write about your ideas and present your text to the class.

20 STUDY SKILLS Your speech ➜ SB (p. 109)

You are going to write a speech for the following event:

You are at a conference[1] with young people from different countries. Together you want to organize protests and call for stricter international policies to protect the environment. You are going to give a short speech on an issue that is important to you, e.g. protecting a certain region, saving certain animals from extinction or starting a campaign that you think is absolutely necessary.

STEP 1: Plan your speech.

a) Write down your topic: ______________________________

b) Make notes for the different parts in your exercise book.

1 **Addressing the audience:** Your listeners are young people like you and you all have common interests. Think of a fitting way to start your speech.

2 **Waking interest:** Explain in a few sentences why the issue you have chosen is important. Give some general information so your audience is introduced to your topic and understands your intentions.

3 **Main body:** Go into detail, giving facts and good examples. Start with the most important fact. Put the information in a logical order. You could use some stylistic devices, such as alliteration, contrast and repetition.

4 **Making an appeal:** Suggest what action you should take together.

5 **Closing:** Summarize the main aspects of your speech in a few sentences. Appeal to your audience again to take a stand on the issue.

STEP 2: Draft your speech. Then give each other feedback.

STEP 3: Edit and improve your speech. Type it on a computer.

STEP 4: Give your speech. Record it or read it to your partner or class. If you feel confident, only use some notes.

[1]conference ['kɒnfrns] *Konferenz*

21 Native English speakers and other languages
➜ SB (p. 110) • Wordbank 7

a) ● Since English is a lingua franca, it is easy for native speakers to communicate in lots of countries. Find out what effect that has on their foreign language education.

Research the language-learning situation in schools in these countries and take notes:

1 The UK: ____________________

____

____

2 The US: ____________________

____

____

3 Australia: ____________________

____

____

4 New Zealand: ____________________

____

____

b) Compare your results and discuss possible reasons for the language-learning situation in the four countries.

22 Comparing translations
➜ SB (p. 111) • SMC 32 (p. 86)

a) The English text below is the beginning of a story by Katherine Mansfield, a famous writer from New Zealand. Compare it with the two translations.

- Which German version was translated by a professional translator and which by a machine? Give reasons.
- What is your impression of the quality of the text that was translated by a machine?

And after all the weather was ideal. They could not have had a more perfect day for a garden-party if they had ordered it. Windless, warm, the sky without a cloud.	Und das Wetter war ja auch ideal. Einen perfekteren Tag für eine Gartenparty hätten sie nicht haben können, wenn sie ihn bestellt hätten. Windstill, warm, der Himmel ohne eine Wolke.	Und endlich war das Wetter ideal. Für eine Gartenparty hätte es keinen schöneren Tag geben können – es war wie bestellt. Windstill, warm, ein Himmel ohne Wolken.

b) Translate these German sentences with the help of an online dictionary. Write your translations below. Then use at least two different translation machines and compare the results.

1 Das kannst du dir abschminken. ____________________

2 Nun bleib mal auf dem Teppich. ____________________

3 Er ist aus allen Wolken gefallen. ____________________

1 PRONUNCIATION Word stress

a) Say these words from Unit 4 aloud and underline the stressed syllables. You can record your voice.

calendar democracy contribute agriculture rehearse complex visa poetic itinerary

b) 23 Listen and check. Then say the words again.

2 What will they be doing? (Future progressive)

Fill in the future progressive forms of the verbs in brackets. Use short forms.

1 Take your keys with you because I ______________ when you get back. (surf)

2 I've cycled to school for the last few months, but from next week I ______________ the bus. (take)

3 Ava has a new flat. Too bad she ______________ close to us any more. (not live)

4 Emre ______________ at the school concert with his band next week. (play)

3 By the time you visit us ... (Future perfect simple)

Complete the sentences with future perfect forms of the verbs in the box.

arrive · be · not finish · pass

1 By the time you visit us in New Zealand, we ______________ there for more than three months.

2 John is taking driving lessons and hopes he ______________ his test by the end of October.

3 Melanie can't see the earlier film at the cinema because she ______________ work yet.

4 Let's call Mum and Dad. They ______________ at their hotel in Madrid by now.

4 An introduction to a presentation

This introduction to a presentation is quite confusing. Rewrite it so the audience can easily follow it. Improve the style where necessary.

I've decided to talk about Māori culture today. Oh, I should say good morning first. Hi everybody. Well, my talk has four parts. I'll finish by talking about the positive developments for indigenous people since the late 20th century. Oh, I forgot to say that first I want to tell you about the lives of the Māori when they were the only inhabitants of New Zealand. I've also collected some interesting facts about how Māori culture changed after the British had arrived. The next part is about te reo – that's the Māori's language. Okay, let's start with the coming of the Māori to New Zealand.

____

____

____

____

____

____

5 Referring to pictures, posters and slides

If you include pictures, posters and slides in a presentation, you should refer to them while you are talking. Here are some typical phrases used in different presentations. Complete them with the verbs from the box.

compare · draw · have · look at · notice · see · show

1 The pictures ______________ some early British settlements in New Zealand.

2 Please ______________ the next slide which gives you an impression of Fiordland National Park.

3 As you can ______________ in the photos, New Zealand has rural, tropical and mountainous landscapes.

4 Please ______________ a look at these examples of Māori art.

5 I'd now like to ______________ your attention to a map of the South Pacific region.

6 If you ______________ the two travel adverts, you will certainly ______________ that the design differs.

6 A short talk ➜ *Wordbanks 7-8*

Give a three-minute talk on this topic:

English and other lingua francas

Use the information on p. 110 of your student's book and find some other facts. You could structure your talk like this:

- Introduce your topic and give an outline of your talk.
- Explain why English became a lingua franca.
- Give examples of where and when English is used.
- List advantages and disadvantages of English as a lingua franca.
- Give some examples of other global languages that are important in certain parts of the world.
- Draw conclusions from your comparisons.
- Sum up your main points.

Check: Speaking

a) Vergleiche deine Antworten mit den Lösungen auf Seite 88 in diesem Workbook.
b) Schätze deine Antworten mit einem grünen oder roten Gesicht ein.

	☺	☹	
1 PRONUNCIATION Word stress Konntest du die Wörter problemlos richtig aussprechen?	○	○	➜ 1
4 An introduction to a presentation Kannst du gut strukturiert in das Thema eines Vortrags einführen?	○	○	➜ 5
5 Referring to pictures, posters and slides Kennst du wichtige Ausdrücke, die man immer wieder in Präsentationen verwendet?	○	○	➜ 2
6 A short talk Konntest du wichtige Informationen finden und den Vortrag sinnvoll aufbauen?	○	○	➜ 3, 4, 5

c) Wenn du dich mit rot eingeschätzt hast, schau dir die rechte Spalte an. Die Nummern führen dich zu den passenden Übungen im Skills Training (S. 62-63). Dort kannst du gezielt das Sprechen trainieren.

1 PRONUNCIATION Word stress

a) Say these words and mark the stressed syllables.

1 identity	4 repetition	7 campaign	10 resources
2 signature	5 economy	8 politician	11 petition
3 intensive	6 category	9 chemical	12 tourism

TIP: Word stress is important for meaning. It is often different in German. Use a dictionary to check. Remember:
' = main stress
ˌ = secondary stress
activist ['æktɪvɪst]
interviewee [ˌɪntəvju'iː]

b) 24 Listen and check. Then say the words again.

2 Useful phrases for presentations

Complete these signposting phrases for presentations.

TIP: Your listeners can follow you more easily if the structure of your talk is clear to them. That is why signposting phrases are important.

1 **Greeting the audience:** Good ____________ . It's nice ____________ .

2 **Dealing with interruptions:** If you have any questions, ____________ .

3 **Beginning a part:** First I'd ____________ the early history of New Zealand.

4 **Going on to a new part:** Now I'd like to ____________ about the Polynesian settlers.

5 **Giving extra information:** Let me ____________ this aspect by ____________ you ____________ .

6 **Summing up:** Let me ____________ you of some of the ____________ we've ____________ .

7 **Closing your talk:** That ____________ us to the ____________ of my talk. Thank you ____________ .

3 Practising a talk → *SMC 25 (p. 84)* • *Wordbank 8*

a) Practise talking about the importance of several global languages. Use the table below. You could start like this:

Not only English is a lingua franca. There are also some other languages that are important in certain parts of the world. Arabic, for example, is ...

TIP: It is helpful to practise a talk several times, e.g. in front of a mirror. If you record your talk, you can check whether you have spoken fluently.

Global language	Where it is spoken	Native and second-language speakers
Arabic	official language in many North African and Middle Eastern countries; trade language in many other African countries	about 350 million people (all varieties of Arabic)
French	official language in France and many of its former[1] colonies; lingua franca in most Western and Central African countries; second most used language in politics, diplomacy and culture	almost 275 million people
Mandarin Chinese	official language and lingua franca of China and Taiwan, where many other dialects of Chinese are spoken	over 1.1 billion people
Russian	official language in Russia and three other Eastern European states; lingua franca in large parts of Eastern Europe and in Central Asia	about 260 million people
Spanish	official language in Spain and 19 other countries; second most used language in international trade; third most used language in politics, diplomacy and culture	nearly 600 million people

b) Record your talk. Then listen to it. Are you pleased with it? If not, try again.

[1] former ['fɔːmə] *ehemalig*

4 A conclusion

These sentences make up a conclusion of a presentation. Number them in a logical order.

TIP: You only have to repeat the most important points of a talk in a conclusion.

- ☐ Thank you for your attention.
- ☐ In addition, some languages are still widely used in international politics and diplomacy.
- ☐ As English is spoken by more than one billion native and second-language speakers around the world, it will probably remain the most important lingua franca.
- ☐ As I've pointed out in my talk, I think that due to globalisation more students should learn a third language that is almost as important as English.
- ☐ To sum up, there are several different languages that serve as lingua francas.
- ☐ However, as we've seen, there are large regions where other languages are very important.

5 English in your life

➜ *SMC 25 (p. 84)* • *Wordbank 8*

TIP: A table helps you to order your points so that your talk has a logical structure. Your listeners will understand it better.

Prepare a short talk about your experiences of learning English and using it in different situations. Then record it.

a) Collect ideas and make notes in the table.

Aspects	Notes
How long I have been learning English	
My experiences with English at school	
What I need English for in my free time	
Situations in which I used English as a lingua franca	
What motivates me to improve my English	
What discourages me when studying and using English	
The importance of English for my personal future	

b) Make notes for the introduction and the conclusion.

- Introduction: ______________________

____

- Conclusion: ______________________

____

1 Talking about the present ➜ SB (p. 142)

1.1 The simple present

We use the **simple present** to say that something happens **regularly, often, always** or **never.**
We often use it with phrases of time like *always, never, often, sometimes, usually, every week, on Fridays, after school,* etc.

- *Jack **usually gets** the bus to school.* *Jack **nimmt** meistens den Bus zur Schule.*
- ***On Fridays** his mother **takes** him in the car.* *Freitags **bringt** ihn seine Mutter mit dem Auto.*

We also use the **simple present** to make **general statements.**

- *Olivia **lives** in Chester.* *Olivia **wohnt** in Chester.*
- *Her parents **work** for a computer company.* *Ihre Eltern **arbeiten** für eine Computerfirma.*

1.2 The present progressive

We use the **present progressive** to say that someone is **doing something now** or that something is **happening now.**
The action or event is **not finished yet.** Common phrases of time are *at the moment, now, just* and *still.*

- *What**'s** Dan **doing**? He**'s cleaning** his bike.* *Was **macht** Dan? Er **putzt** sein Rad.*
- *Dan (on the phone): "I'm busy, Oliver. I**'m** still **cleaning** my bike."*
  *„Ich bin beschäftigt, Oliver. Ich **bin** noch **dabei**, mein Rad **zu putzen**."*

We also use the **present progressive** for actions that are repeated over a limited period of time.

- *Olivia has a holiday job. She**'s working** as a waitress in a café in Devon. She**'s living** with her aunt while she's there.*
  *… Sie **arbeitet** als Kellnerin in einem Café in Devon. Während sie sich dort aufhält, **wohnt** sie bei ihrer Tante.*

1.3 Simple present or present progressive?

In German, ***Harry und Ben spielen Hockey*** can mean two things:

a) Playing hockey is Harry and Ben's hobby.

In English, we use the **simple present** for meaning **a):**

- *Harry and Ben **play** hockey every Friday.*

b) They are in the middle of a hockey match.

We use the **present progressive** for meaning **b):**

- *Harry and Ben **are playing** hockey at the moment.*

2 Talking about the past (I) ➜ SB (p. 144)

2.1 The simple past

We use the **simple past** to say that something happened **in the past** (it is now over). Time phrases like *last Friday, yesterday, last week, in 2012, ten years ago* and *an hour ago* are often used.

- *Olivia's mother **moved** to England **ten years ago**.*
  *Vor zehn Jahren **ist** Olivias Mutter nach England **gezogen / zog** Olivias Mutter nach England.*

We use the simple past in **reports** about past events and in **stories** (often with *first …, then …, after that …).*

- *Yesterday Olivia **went** to town with her friend Sue. They **tried** on shoes in four shops, but they **didn't buy** any.*

2.2 *used to* + infinitive / *would* + infinitive (German "früher")

With ***used to* + infinitive** we can talk about things that were true in the past but are not true any more.

- *We **used to live** in Manchester.* *Wir **wohnten früher** in Manchester.*
- *He **didn't use to be** so shy, did he?* *Er **war früher** nicht so schüchtern, oder?*

We can also use ***would* + infinitive** (without *to)* to talk about **regular actions** in the past.

- *We **would** often **go** for long walks in the woods.*
  *Wir **haben** oft lange Spaziergänge im Wald **gemacht**. / Wir **pflegten** lange Spaziergänge im Wald **zu machen**.*

2.3 The past progressive

We use the **past progressive** to talk about actions that were **not yet finished** at a particular time in the past.

- *Yesterday at 3:30 Olivia **was waiting** for her bus.* *Gestern um 15.30 **wartete** Olivia noch auf ihren Bus.*

The simple past is used with the **past progressive** when a short action interrupts a **longer action.**

- *Sally **was cycling** home when a dog ran out in front of her bike.*
  *Sally **radelte (gerade)** nach Hause, als ihr ein Hund vors Fahrrad **lief**.*

3 Talking about the past (II) ➜ *SB (p. 146)*

3.1 The past perfect (simple)

To talk about a past action, we use the simple past, e.g.
- *Emily got home.*
- *It started to rain.*

To say what happened before a past action, we use the **past perfect.**
- *When Emily got home, her parents **had already eaten**.* *Als Emily nach Hause kam, **hatten** ihre Eltern **schon gegessen**.*
- *We **had already arrived** home when it started to rain.* *Wir **waren schon** zu Hause **angekommen,** als es anfing zu regnen.*

3.2 The past perfect progressive

We use the past perfect (simple) to say what happened before a past action.
- *We **had** already **arrived** home when it started to rain.*

We use the **past perfect progressive** for *continuous* actions that ended at (or just before) a past point of time.
- *We **had been playing** tennis for half an hour when it started to rain.*
  *Wir **hatten** eine halbe Stunde Tennis **gespielt,** als es anfing zu regnen.*
- *Olivia was very tired when she arrived home. She **had been studying** for a test all day.*
  *Olivia war sehr müde, als sie nach Hause kam. Sie **hatte** den ganzen Tag für einen Test **gelernt**.*

4 Linking the past and the present ➜ *SB (p. 148)*

4.1 The present perfect (simple)

We use the **present perfect (simple)** when a **past** action has a connection with *now*.
1. *Mel **has lost** her mobile. She can't phone anyone.* *Mel **hat** ihr Handy **verloren**. Sie kann niemanden anrufen.*
2. *I think Matt Damon is great. I**'ve seen** all his films.* *Ich finde Matt Damon toll. Ich **habe** alle seine Filme **gesehen**.*
3. *Luke must be hungry. He **hasn't eaten yet** today.* *Luke muss hungrig sein. Er **hat** heute noch nichts **gegessen**.*
4. ***Have** you **ever been** to Paris? – No, I**'ve never been** there, but I'd like to go.*
   Warst du schon (mal) in Paris? – Nein, ich war noch nie dort, aber ich würde gern hinfahren.

4.2 The present perfect progressive

We use the **present perfect progressive** for actions that **began in the past** and have continued till **now.**
1. *Ella **has been writing** letters **all afternoon**.* *Ella schreibt (schon) den ganzen Nachmittag Briefe.*
2. *My brother **has been playing** the piano **since** 2013.* *Mein Bruder spielt seit 2013 Klavier.*
3. ***How long have** you **been learning** French now?* *Wie lange lernst du jetzt (schon) Französisch?*

The **present perfect progressive** in these sentences corresponds to the German *Präsens:*
- *He**'s been playing** … since/for …* *Er **spielt** seit …*

Some common time phrases are *all afternoon, all day, the whole morning, since …, for …*

4.3 *since* and *for:* German "seit"

***since* + Zeitpunkt** (wann etwas begann)	***for* + Zeitraum** (wie lange etwas andauert)
*I've been playing the drums **since 2015**.* *… seit 2015*	*I've been playing the piano **for three years**.* *… seit drei Jahren*

4.4 Present perfect or present perfect progressive?

When we say *how long* something has been happening: ***present perfect progressive***.

When we talk about the result of an action: ***present perfect (simple)***.

- *Ella **has been writing** letters **all afternoon**.*
  *Ella **schreibt** (schon) den ganzen Nachmittag Briefe.*
- *Ella **has written** three letters since lunch.*
  *Ella **hat** seit dem Mittagessen drei Briefe **geschrieben**.*

5 Talking about the past: tenses in contrast ➜ SB (p. 150)

5.1 Present perfect or simple past?

With the **present perfect (simple)**, we talk about actions and events that happened at some time in the past. The exact time is not important (or not known) and is not mentioned. The action or event often has a connection with *now*.
- *Look, I'**ve bought** a new pair of jeans. They'll go well with my red top.*
- *Luke **has** already **done** his maths homework, but he **hasn't started** his French yet.*
- ***Have** you ever **been** a member of a sports club? – No, never. But I'd like to join one now.*

With the **simple past**, we say that something happened at a particular point of time in the past or in a particular period of time in the past (which is now over).
- *We **went** to the new cinema last weekend.*
- *What year **did** you **start** school?*

5.2 Simple past or past perfect?

With the **simple past**, we talk about past actions:
- *The Millers **arrived** at the campsite at 11 pm.*
- *I **visited** Mary in hospital last week.*

With the **past perfect (simple)**, we say what happened before a past action.
- *The restaurant **had** already **closed** when the Millers **arrived** at the campsite.* … ***hatte** bereits **geschlossen** …*
- *When I **visited** Mary in hospital, she **had** already **been** there for two weeks.* … ***war** sie schon zwei Wochen dort …*

6 Talking about the future (I) ➜ SB (p. 152)

6.1 The *going to*-future

We use the ***going to*-future** to talk about **intentions** or **plans** for the future.
- *After school I'**m going to study** architecture.*
  *Nach der Schule **werde** ich Architektur **studieren** / **habe** ich **vor**, Architektur **zu studieren**.*
- *The Millers **are going to move** to New Zealand.*
  *Die Millers **werden** nach Neuseeland **ziehen** / **wollen** nach Neuseeland **ziehen**.*

We use the ***going to*-future** to make predictions about the future, especially when you can already see the signs.
- *Look at those clouds. There's **going to be** a storm.* *Schau dir die Wolken an. Es **wird** ein Gewitter **geben**.*
- *Oops! It looks like I'**m going to be** in trouble.* *Huch! Ich glaube, das **wird** Ärger **geben**.*

6.2 The *will*-future

We use the ***will*-future** to make statements or predictions about the future.

We often use it when talking about things that we **cannot control** (e.g. our age, the weather).
- *I'**ll be** 16 next October.* *Nächsten Oktober **werde** ich 16.*
- *It **will be** cool tomorrow.* *Morgen **wird** es kühl **sein/werden**.*
- *There **will be** showers in the west.* *Im Westen **wird** es Schauer **geben**.*

When we make predictions, we often use these expressions: *I think, I'm sure, I suppose, I expect, I hope, maybe, probably.*
- ***I suppose** Ella **will arrive** late again as usual.* ***Ich nehme an,** Ella kommt wie üblich wieder zu spät.*
- *Dan **will probably feel** tired when he gets in.* *Dan wird **wahrscheinlich** müde sein, wenn er nach Hause kommt.*

We use the ***will*-future** when we decide something in the moment we speak, e.g. when we make a **promise** or an **offer.**
- *I **won't tell** anyone what's happened.* *Ich **sage** niemandem/ **werde** niemandem **sagen**, was passiert ist.*
- *One moment – I'**ll open** the door for you.* *Moment. Ich **mache** Ihnen die Tür **auf**.*

6.3 The future perfect (*will* + *have* + past participle)

We use the **future perfect** to say something will be **complete at a future point of time** (e.g. next Friday, by the end of the month, etc.).
- ***Next Friday we will have finished** the exams.* *Nächsten Freitag **werden** wir die Prüfungen **geschafft haben**.*
- ***By the end of the week we'll have got** the results.* *Bis Ende der Woche **werden** wir die Ergebnisse **erhalten haben**.*

7 Talking about the future (II) ➜ *SB (p. 154)*

7.1 The future progressive (*will* + *be* + *-ing*-form)

We use the **future progressive** for actions that will be **in progress at a point of time in the future.**
We often use it with phrases of time like *a week today* ("heute in einer Woche") and *this time next week*.
- *A week today Jana will be in Spain – and I**'ll be doing** my maths exam.*
  *Heute in einer Woche wird Jana in Spanien sein – und ich **werde dabei sein**, meine Mathe-Prüfung **zu machen**.*

We often use the **future progressive** when we **expect** something to happen or **know** that it will happen.
- *We**'ll be playing** football again next Friday.* *Nächsten Freitag **spielen** wir **(wie immer)** Fußball.*
- *I**'ll be going** shopping later. Do you need anything?* *Ich **gehe (ohnehin)** nachher einkaufen. Brauchst du etwas?*

We also use the **future progressive** to ask politely about somebody's plans.
- *What **will** you **be doing** over the next couple of days?* *Was **werden** Sie die nächsten Tage **unternehmen**?*

7.2 The present progressive

We use the **present progressive** to say that something is **definitely planned or arranged** for the future.
- *I**'m meeting** a friend in town **tomorrow** at 12.*
- *All my friends **are coming** to my party **on Friday**.*

We need a future time phrase *(tomorrow, on Friday)* unless the context shows that a sentence is about the future.
- *Can we meet up at the weekend? – Sorry, but we**'re driving** to Scotland to see my mum.*

7.3 Overview: *going to*-future, future progressive and present progressive

There are many situations in which the differences between these verb forms do not matter.
However, there are small differences in meaning, and these may be important sometimes. Compare:
- *I feel a bit tired so I**'m going to stay** at home this evening.* ► *You want to stress that you've <u>decided</u>.*
- *I**'ll be staying** at home this evening – my favourite TV series is on.* ► *You're talking about a <u>routine</u>.*
- *I can't meet you today. We've invited some friends, so I**'m staying** at home.* ► *You want to stress you have an <u>arrangement</u>.*

7.4 The simple present

We use the **simple present** when a future event is part of a **timetable, schedule** or **programme.**
Verbs like *arrive, leave, go, open, close, start, stop* are often used in this way.
- *When **does** the next train to Liverpool **leave**?* *Wann **fährt** der nächste Zug nach Liverpool?*
- *Our cookery course **starts** on 2 September.* *Unser Kochkurs **startet** am 2. September.*

8 Aspect: The simple form and the progressive form ➜ *SB (p. 156)*

8.1 Simple and progressive form compared

In contrast to German, English verbs have **simple forms** and **progressive forms.**

Tense	Simple form	Progressive form
Present tense	**sing(s)**	**am/are/is singing**
Past tense	**sang**	**was/were singing**
Present perfect	**have/has sung**	**have/has been singing**
Past perfect	**had sung**	**had been singing**
***will*-future**	**will sing**	**will be singing**

We use the **simple form** to say that
- someone does something regularly or repeatedly ► *Tom **plays** basketball on Saturdays.* ► It's his hobby.
- an action is long-lasting or permanent ► *Mr Clark **works** as an editor.* ► It's his job.
- an action is complete. ► *Sue **has written** four letters today.* ► She has finished.

We use the **progressive form** to say that
- an action is in progress at the moment of speaking ► *Tom isn't in. He**'s playing** basketball.* ► right now
- an action is going on for a temporary period of time ► *This week Mr Clark **is working** in London.* ► just this week
- an action is not yet complete. ► *Sue **has been writing** letters all day.* ► she's still writing

8.2 Activity verbs and state verbs

Activity verbs refer to **activities** *(do, go, make, read, …)* or **events** *(become, happen, rain, …)*.
They can be used both in the **simple form** and in the **progressive form.**

- *(in a shop window) We **make** the best pizza in town!*
- *It **gets** dark very early here in winter.*
- *(on the phone) I'm **making** pizza. I'll call you back.*
- *At 5 o'clock it **was** already **getting** dark.*

State verbs do not refer to **activities.** They refer to **states.**

State verbs are used only in the **simple form.** They can refer to

1 **characteristics and ownership:** *be, exist, include, seem, sound, mean* ("bedeuten"), *cost, need, own, belong, …*
- *Emily **seems** happy at her new school now.* not … ~~is seeming~~ …
- *The price **doesn't include** breakfast.* not … ~~isn't including~~ …
- *Jake's uncle **owns** a house in the country.* not … ~~is owning~~ …

2 **thinking and knowing:** *believe, know, mean* ("meinen"), *remember, imagine, realize, recognize, understand, …*
- ***Do** you **believe** their story?* not … ~~Are you believing …~~
- *I **don't know** the answer to question 5.* not … ~~I'm not knowing~~ …
- *Anna **didn't understand** what Julie **meant**.* not … ~~wasn't understanding~~ … ~~was meaning~~

3 **liking, disliking and wishing:** *like, love, dislike, hate, mind, prefer, want, wish, …*
- *Lucy **doesn't like** people who talk a lot.* not … ~~isn't liking~~ …
- *I **don't mind** waiting for you here.* not … ~~I'm not minding~~ …
- *We **prefer** brown bread to white bread.* not … ~~are preferring~~

9 The passive (I) ➜ SB (p. 158)

9.1 Active and passive

Verbs can be **active** or **passive**. Which one you use depends on the focus of your sentence.

- **Active:** *In 1971, **John Lennon wrote** "Imagine".* *Im Jahr 1971 schrieb John Lennon „Imagine".*
- **Passive:** ***"Imagine" was written** in 1971.* *„Imagine" wurde im Jahr 1971 geschrieben.*

► The **active** sentence is about **John Lennon.** It tells us what he did in 1971.

► The **passive** sentence is about **"Imagine".** It tells us when the song was written.

9.2 The passive: use

We use the passive to say what is done or what happens to something or someone.
Who does the action is often unknown or unimportant (1 and 2) or obvious (3 and 4).

1 *The match **was cancelled** because of rain.* *Das Spiel **wurde** wegen Regen **abgesagt.***
2 *A new sports centre **has been opened** in Chelsea.* *In Chelsea **ist** ein neues Sportzentrum **eröffnet worden.***
3 *Breakfast **is served** from 7 to 10:30 am.* *Frühstück **wird** von 7 bis 10.30 **serviert.***
4 *The thieves **have been sentenced** to two years.* *Die Diebe **sind** zu zwei Jahren Haft **verurteilt worden.***

The passive is often found in reports of accidents, crimes or natural disasters and in technical or scientific writing.

> Yesterday a drunk driver hit a 15-year-old boy in Lichfield Road. The boy was taken to hospital, where he was treated for shock. He is now recovering. The driver was taken to Horton Road police station. He is answering police questions.

! Often, we change between **active** and **passive** so that we can focus on one person or thing over several sentences (here: the 15-year-old boy).

> Yesterday a drunk driver **hit** a 15-year-old boy … The boy **was taken** to hospital, where he **was treated** … He **is** now **recovering**.

If you want to say who or what does the action, you can use the preposition **by**.
- *The driver **was questioned by the police**.* *Der Fahrer wurde von der Polizei verhört/befragt.*
- *The house **was damaged by a falling tree**.* *Das Haus wurde von einem umstürzenden Baum beschädigt.*

10 The passive (II) ➔ *SB (p. 160)*

10.1 The passive: form

In German, the passive is a form of "werden" + past participle. In English, it is a **form of *be* + past participle.**

Simple present	*English **is spoken** in many countries.*
Simple past	*The match **was talked about** all over Britain.*
Present perfect	*All the biscuits **have been eaten**.*
Past perfect	*I didn't go to the party because I **hadn't been invited.***
***going to*-future**	*Look, the lions **are going to be fed** soon.*
***will*-future and modal auxiliaries**	*The last match of the season **will be played** next Friday.* *Mobile phones **should be turned off** during lessons.* *Concert tickets **can be bought** online.*
Future perfect	*I'm sure lots of new planets **will have been discovered** by 2050.*

The **passive progressive** is formed with ***being***.

Present progressive	*Three new blocks of flats **are being built** in King Street.*
Past progressive	*The museum was closed. The rooms **were being painted.***

10.2 The passive of verbs with two objects

Some verbs can have **two objects,** e.g.
- *give/promise/send/show **somebody** something* ***jemandem etwas*** *geben/versprechen/schicken/zeigen*

In English, **passive sentences** with verbs like these usually begin with the person (***She*** …).
This structure is called **personal passive** ("persönliches Passiv").

	object object	**object object**
Active	*The manager promised **her a job.***	*Der Manager versprach **ihr eine Stelle.***
Passive	***She*** (subject) *was promised **a job*** (object).	***Ihr*** (indirect object, dative) *wurde **eine Stelle*** (subject) *versprochen.*

Personal passive sentences are very common in English. In German, you have to use other constructions.
- ***She was paid** a lot of money for her book.*
  Ihr wurde eine Menge Geld gezahlt für ihr Buch./ Sie bekam eine Menge Geld für ihr Buch.
- ***He was given** the key and went up to his room.* *Ihm wurde der Schlüssel gegeben …/ Er bekam den Schlüssel …*
- ***I've been told** she has lost her job.* *Mir wurde erzählt, dass sie ihre Stelle verloren hat.*

11 Modal auxiliaries ➜ SB (p. 162)

11.1 Use

The modal auxiliaries are *can, could, may,* etc.

can	*could*	*may*	*might*	*must*	*mustn't*
needn't	*ought to*	*shall*	*should*	*will*	*would*

We use modals to talk about whether something is **allowed, possible** or **necessary.**
- *You* ***can*** *take the car. I* ***can*** *go by bike.* *Du* ***darfst*** *das Auto nehmen. Ich* ***kann*** *mit dem Rad fahren.*
- *Do you think we* ***should*** *invite Jake to the party?* *Meinst du, dass wir Jake zur Party einladen* ***sollten****?*
- *I* ***must*** *go shopping. The fridge is nearly empty.* *Ich* ***muss*** *einkaufen gehen. Der Kühlschrank ist fast leer.*

! Note the difference between ***needn't*** and ***mustn't:***
You ***needn't*** *feed the cats. I fed them this morning.*
Du ***musst*** *die Katzen* ***nicht*** *füttern. …*
You ***mustn't*** *feed the horses. It's bad for them.*
Du ***darfst*** *die Pferde* ***nicht*** *füttern. …*

! Compare the different uses of ***shall, should*** and ***ought to*** (German "sollen"):
1. We use ***shall*** to make **suggestions** and **offers:**
   - ***Shall*** *we eat first and go shopping later?* ***Sollen/Wollen*** *wir erst essen …?*
2. We use ***should*** and ***ought to*** to say what is the best or the right thing to do **(advice; obligation).**
   - You ***should/ought to*** *tell him the truth.* *Du* ***solltest*** *ihm die Wahrheit sagen.*

We also use modals to say if we think something may happen, or that something is likely or certain to happen.

1. *There's somebody at the door.*
   - *That* ***may*** *be Julie.* *Das ist* ***vielleicht*** *Julie.*
   - *That* ***could*** *be Julie.* *Das* ***könnte*** *Julie sein.*
   - *That* ***must*** *be Julie.* *Das* ***muss*** *Julie sein.*
   - *That* ***might*** *be Julie.* *Das* ***könnte (vielleicht)*** *Julie sein.*
   - *That* ***will*** *be Julie.* *Das* ***wird*** *Julie sein.*
   - *That* ***can't*** *be Julie.* *Das* ***kann nicht*** *Julie sein.*
2. *Julie* ***should/ought to*** *be here by now.* *Julie* ***sollte*** *jetzt (eigentlich) hier sein.*
3. *I* ***must*** *have fallen asleep.* *Ich* ***muss*** *eingeschlafen sein.*

11.2 Form

1. There is **one form of modal for all persons** (no *-s*-forms, no *-ing*-forms). It is used with an **infinitive.**
   - ***I/We can/could/…*** ***help*** *you with those bags now.*
   - ***He/She/They can/could/…*** ***help*** *you …*
2. We do not use *do/does/did* to make negative sentences or questions. In short answers, modals can stand on their own.
   - ***Jack can't help*** *you today. –* ***Can*** *he* ***help*** *me tomorrow? – Yes, he* ***can****. / No, he* ***can't****.*
3. Modals cannot form most of the verb tenses. There is no *-ed*-form. That is why we have to use **substitute forms.**

12 Modals and their substitutes ➜ SB (p. 164)

Some modals have **substitute forms,** which we need to form the **infinitive,** the ***-ing*-form** and **other tenses.**
- *I'd love* ***to be able*** *to play the piano.* *Ich würde liebend gern Klavier spielen* ***können****.*
- ***Being able to*** *play the piano must be great.* *Es muss großartig sein, Klavier spielen* ***zu können****.*
- *We* ***weren't allowed to*** *play the piano after 9 pm.* *Wir* ***durften*** *nach 21 Uhr* ***nicht*** *Klavier spielen.*
- *You* ***won't be allowed to*** *play the piano after 9 pm.* *Nach 21 Uhr* ***wirst*** *du* ***nicht*** *Klavier spielen* ***dürfen****.*

Here is an overview of modals and their substitutes in different tenses.

German "können": modal auxiliary *can* – modal substitute *(to) be able to*

Present	*My little brother* ***can/is able to*** *swim. My cousins* ***can't/aren't able to*** *swim.*
Past	***Were*** *you* ***able to*** *visit the British Museum when you were in London?* *I* ***could*** *smell fire, but I* ***couldn't*** *see any smoke.*
Present perfect	*I* ***haven't been able to*** *contact Jack yet. Do you think he* ***has been able to*** *check his mails?*
***will*-future**	*I'm taking driving lessons, so next year I'****ll be able to*** *drive.*

German "dürfen": modal auxiliary *can*/*may* – modal substitute *(to) be allowed to*

Present	***Can*/*May*** *I have a sleepover on Friday, Mum?* *Jake **is allowed to** stay up late in the week, but we **aren't (allowed to)**.*
Past	*Under-12s **couldn't**/**weren't allowed to** see the film without an adult.*
Present perfect	***I've** always **been allowed to** have pets.*
***will*-future**	***Will** you **be allowed to** go to the party?*

German "müssen": modal auxiliary *must* – modal substitute *(to) have to*

Present	Teacher: *You **must** work harder, Noah.* *Noah's teacher says he **has to** work harder.* *I **needn't** get up at 6 tomorrow./I **don't have to** get up at 6 tomorrow.*
Past	*I **had to** rewrite my essay, but we **didn't have to** do any maths homework.*
Present perfect	*Lauren **has had to** go to the dentist's a lot recently.*
***will*-future**	*You **will have to** go to the dentist's too if you don't look after your teeth better.*

13 The to-infinitive ➜ *SB (p. 166)*

13.1 Verb + object + *to*-infinitive

We can use an **object** + ***to*-infinitive** after *cause, expect, tell, want, would like, would love.*
- *His parents **expect him to be** home by ten.* *Seine Eltern erwarten, **dass** er bis zehn Uhr zu Hause ist.*
- *The police officer **told us to wait** outside.* *Die Polizeibeamtin sagte, **dass** wir draußen warten sollten.*
- ***I'd like you to sit** down in a circle now.* *Ich möchte, **dass** ihr euch jetzt im Kreis hinsetzt.*

! After the German verbs, there is usually a clause with **"dass".** In English, a ***that*-clause** is **not possible.**

Other verbs that can take an **object** + ***to*-infinitive** include *allow, ask, help, invite, teach.*
- *Our teacher **allows us to use** mobiles.* *Unser Lehrer erlaubt uns, Handys **zu benutzen**.*
- *My sister **asked me not to wear** her T-shirts.* *Meine Schwester bat mich, nicht ihre T-Shirts **zu tragen**.*
- *Pictures can **help you to learn** new words.* *Bilder können dir helfen, neue Wörter **zu lernen**.*

13.2 Question word + *to*-infinitive

After question words *(what, who, …),* we can use subordinate clauses with modal auxiliaries *(can, must, …).*

• *I don't know*	***what I can do***	***who I must ask***	***where I should go.***
Ich weiß nicht,	*was ich tun kann*	*wen ich fragen muss*	*wohin ich gehen soll.*

! However, a ***to*-infinitive is the more usual structure in English. (It is not possible in German.)**

• *I don't know*	*what **to do***	*who **to ask***	*where **to go.***

13.3 The *to*-infinitive instead of a relative clause

We often use a ***to*-infinitive** instead of a ***relative clause***.
It can come after a **superlative (1)** and after ***the first, the last, the next, the only*** **(2–4).**
1. ***Sophie was the youngest (girl) to take** part.* ► *… the youngest (girl) **who took** part.*
2. *The **first/last person to arrive** was Jonathan.* ► *The first/last person **who arrived** …*
3. *We're the **only shop to offer** this service. …* ► *the only shop **that offers** this service.*
4. *I was **the only person/the only one to win** a prize.* ► *… the only person/the only one **who won** a prize.*

! ***the only*** must be followed by a noun *(shop, person, …)* or *one/ones.*

The *to*-infinitive can also come after a **noun** (especially ***person, place, way***). It replaces a **relative clause with a modal.**
- *Luigi's is **the place to go** for a good pizza.* ► *… the place **that you must/should go to** …*
- *I'm looking for **someone to share** a flat with.* ► *… someone **who I can share** a flat with.*

It can also replace a **relative clause** after ***someone, anybody, something, anything, nothing, nowhere,*** etc.
- *There's **nothing to do** and **nowhere to go**.* ► *There's nothing **that I can do** and nowhere **that I can go**.*

14 Conditional sentences ➜ SB (p. 168)

A conditional sentence tells us what must happen so that something else can happen too.
***If you give me your number*, *I'll call you*.** *Wenn du mir deine Nummer gibst, rufe ich dich an.*

Conditional sentences have a **subordinate clause** with *if* and a **main clause.** There are three common types of sentence.

14.1 Conditional 1: *if* + simple present

In the main clause we can use

the ***will*-future**	*If I **miss** the bus, I'**ll take** a taxi.* *Wenn ich den Bus verpasse, nehme ich ein Taxi.*
a **modal**	*If Dan **misses** the bus, he **can**/**should**/**must take** a taxi.*
an **imperative**	*If you **miss** the bus, **take** a taxi.*

14.2 Conditional 2: *if* + simple past

We use *if* + simple past when we imagine what **might or might not** happen now or in the future.

In the main clause we can use

would + infinitive	*If I **missed** the bus, I'**d take** a taxi.* *Wenn ich den Bus verpasste/verpassen würde, würde ich ein Taxi nehmen.*
could/might + infinitive	*If Dan **missed** the bus, he **could**/**might take** a taxi.*

14.3 Conditional 3: *if* + past perfect

We use *if* + past perfect when we imagine situations that did not happen in the past.
You say *If I had missed the bus ...* only when you did not miss it.

In the main clause we can use

would have + past participle		*If I **had missed** the bus, I **would have taken** a taxi.* *Wenn ich den Bus verpasst hätte, hätte ich ein Taxi genommen.*	
could have ***might have***	+ past participle	*If Dan **had missed** the bus,*	*he **could have taken** a taxi.* *he **might have taken** a taxi.*

14.4 Other conditional sentences

As in German, there can be situations where we use **other combinations of verb forms** in conditional sentences.
- *If I **knew** her better, I **would have asked** her.*
  Wenn ich sie besser kennen würde, hätte ich sie gefragt.
- *If you'**ve been** here before, you'**ll know** the rules.*
  Wenn du schon mal hier warst, dann kennst du (ja) die Regeln.
- *If they **left** at seven, they **won't be** here until twelve.*
  Wenn sie um 7 Uhr losgefahren sind, werden sie erst um 12 hier sein.

15 Relative clauses ➜ SB (p. 170)

15.1 Defining relative clauses

A **defining relative** clause gives **important information** about a noun. (It *defines* the noun.)
- *Do you know the girl **who works at the Oxfam shop**?* *... das Mädchen, **das im Oxfam-Shop arbeitet?***
- *It's the shop **which sells old clothes and books**.* *...der Laden, **der alte Kleidung und Bücher verkauft**.*

We use the relative pronoun *who* for people and *which* for things. We can also use *that* for people and things.
... the girl who works/*... the girl that* works ... *... the shop which* sells .../*... the shop that* sells ...

In English there is **no comma** between the main clause and a defining relative clause.

15.2 Contact clauses

When the **relative pronoun** is the object of the relative clause, we often **leave it out.** This is called a **contact clause.**
You cannot make contact clauses when the relative pronoun is the subject of the relative clause.

	Relative clause
Mr Jones is the teacher	***who I like the most.***
These are the photos	***that Dad took in Wales.***
Do you know the girl	*who* works at the Oxfam shop?

	Relative clause
Mr Jones is the teacher	***I like the most.***
These are the photos	***Dad took in Wales.***

The **relative pronoun** is the subject when the next word is a **verb**, e.g., *the girl* ***who works*** *… / the shop* ***which sells*** *…*

15.3 Non-defining relative clauses

Non-defining relative clauses give **additional information** about a noun. They are used mainly in written English.
- *Agatha Christie,* ***who died in 1976,*** *wrote about 70 detective novels.*
- *John Lennon,* ***whose mother taught him to play the banjo,*** *later became famous as a member of the Beatles.*
- *At 11:35 we landed at Atlanta International,* ***which is one of the world's busiest airports.***

Without a non-defining relative clause, the main clause still makes sense: *At 11:35 we landed at Atlanta International.*

! In non-defining relative clauses:
- you **must** use commas between the relative clause and the main clause
- you **cannot** leave out the relative pronoun
- you **cannot** use the relative pronoun ***that.***

15.4 Relative clauses with *which* to refer to a whole clause

We can use relative clauses with ***which*** to **comment on** the statement in the main clause.
These are like German relative clauses with "was". There is a comma between the main clause and the relative clause.
- *Jane helped us to tidy up,* ***which was very good of her.*** ***…, was ich sehr nett von ihr fand.***
- *I'm late,* ***which means I'm going to miss the train.*** ***…, was bedeutet, dass ich den Zug verpassen werde.***
- *In 1980 John Lennon was murdered,* ***which shocked the world.*** ***…, was die Welt schockierte.***

16 Participles (I) ➔ *SB (p. 172)*

16.1 Participle forms

There are two main participle forms:

1 Present participles (*-ing*-ending)	*work* *dance*	→ →	***working*** ***dancing***	*try* *plan*	→ →	***trying*** ***planning***
2 Past participles (*-ed*-ending with regular verbs)	*work* *dance*	→ →	***worked*** ***danced***	*try* *plan*	→ →	***tried*** ***planned***
Irregular verbs have special past participle forms.	*build* *make* *teach*	→ → →	***built*** ***made*** ***taught***	*grow* *see* *write*	→ → →	***grown*** ***seen*** ***written***

16.2 Participle clauses instead of relative clauses

To make sentences shorter, you can often use participle clauses instead of **relative clauses.**

Present participle (for active verbs)	*The city is always full of people* ***looking for a parking space.*** *(The city is always full of people* ***who are looking for a parking space.****)* *The man* ***driving the red car*** *waved at us.* *(The man* ***who was driving the red car*** *waved at us.)*
Past participle (for passive verbs)	*The Eurovision Song Contest is an international event* ***watched by millions of people.*** *(The Eurovision Song Contest is an international event* ***which is watched by millions of people.****)*

16.3 Verb of perception + object + present participle

After verbs like ***feel, hear, listen to, notice, see, smell, spot*** and ***watch*** we can use an **object + present participle**.

1 *We **heard a baby crying**.* *Wir hörten ein Baby weinen.*
2 *He **watched the band rehearsing**.* *Er beobachtete, wie die Band übte. / Er beobachtete die Band beim Üben.*
3 *She **saw someone climbing** on the roof.*
Sie sah jemanden auf das Dach klettern. / Sie sah, wie/dass jemand auf das Dach kletterte.
4 *I **noticed two women arguing** outside.*
Ich bemerkte, dass sich zwei Frauen draußen stritten./Ich bemerkte zwei Frauen, die sich draußen stritten.

We can also use an infinitive after these verbs. The infinitive expresses the idea that **the complete action is perceived from beginning to end.**
- *We **saw him grab** the money and **run** away.* *Wir sahen, wie er sich das Geld schnappte und davonlief.*

17 Participles (II) → SB (p. 174)

17.1 Participle clauses to describe connected actions

We often use **present participle clauses** to talk about different actions which are connected to each other.
In German sentences like these, we use a main clause with ***und*** or a subordinate clause with ***wobei*** or ***indem.***
- *It rains a lot here, **sometimes flooding the roads.***
*Hier regnet es viel **und** manchmal überschwemmt es (dabei) die Straßen.*
- *Last Sunday morning, we stayed in bed, **reading and listening to the radio.***
*Letzten Sonntagmorgen sind wir im Bett geblieben **und** haben gelesen und Radio gehört.*
- *Charlotte ran down the stairs, **losing a shoe.***
*Charlotte rannte die Treppe hinunter, **wobei** sie einen Schuh verlor.*
- ***Using a knife,** she was able to open the door.*
***Indem** sie ein Messer benutzte, konnte sie die Tür öffnen.*

17.2 Participle clauses instead of adverbial clauses of time

After the conjunctions ***after, before, until, when, while*** you can use **participle clauses** instead of **adverbial clauses of time.**

Present participle (for active verbs)
*Jack decided to go on a world tour **after winning the lottery.*** *(Jack decided to go on a world tour **after he (had) won the lottery.**)* *Jack beschloss, eine Weltreise zu machen, nachdem er im Lotto gewonnen hatte.* ***While walking down the street,** Emily saw a huge dog.* *(**While she was walking down the street,** Emily saw a huge dog.)* *Während Emily die Straße hinunterging, sah sie einen riesigen Hund.*
The conjunctions *while* and *when* can be left out if you put the participle clause at the beginning of a sentence. ***Walking down the street,** Emily saw a huge dog.*
! If you start with the main clause, do not leave out the conjunction. Compare: 1 *Emily saw a huge dog **while walking down the street.*** ► Emily was walking down the street. 2 *Emily saw a huge dog **walking down the street.*** ► The dog was walking down the street.

Past participle (for passive verbs)
***When asked why he left school so early,** he said he had wanted to earn money.* *(**When he was asked why he left school so early,** he said he had wanted to earn money.)* *Als er gefragt wurde, warum er so früh die Schule verlassen habe, …*
The participle clause normally comes before the main clause. The conjunction *(when, while)* can be left out. ***Asked why he left school so early,*** he said he had wanted to earn money.
These past participle structures are typical of written English.

18 Participles (III) ➜ SB (p. 176)

18.1 Participle clauses instead of adverbial clauses of reason

You can use participle clauses as an alternative to **adverbial clauses of reason** (clauses with *because*).

Present participle (for active verbs)

- ***Feeling tired***, *I decided to go to bed early.*
  (I decided to go to bed early because I was feeling tired.)
  Weil/Da ich müde war, beschloss ich, früh schlafen zu gehen.

- ***Being a doctor,*** *she knew exactly what to do.*
  (She knew exactly what to do because she's a doctor.)
  Weil/Da sie Ärztin ist, wusste sie genau, was zu tun ist.

- ***Not knowing what to do,*** *she asked for advice.*
  (She asked for advice because she didn't know what to do.)
  Weil/Da sie nicht wusste, was sie tun sollte, bat sie um Rat.

Not being able to swim, he almost drowned.

! You cannot use the conjunction *because* in participle clauses.

~~*Because feeling very tired,*~~ *…* ~~*Because being a doctor,*~~ *…* ~~*Because not knowing what to do,*~~ *…*

Past participle (for passive verbs)

Warned by his wife, *the man was able to escape.*
(The man was able to escape because he had been warned by his wife.)
Von seiner Frau gewarnt, konnte der Mann entkommen./ Weil er von seiner Frau gewarnt wurde/worden war, …

18.2 Other participle clauses

Participle clauses can begin with other conjunctions, e.g. ***although, if, unless, whether.***

- *It is forbidden to enter the building site* ***unless wearing*** *a hard hat.*
  (It is forbidden to enter the building site unless you are wearing a hard hat.)
  …, außer, man trägt einen Schutzhelm.

- ***Although asked to stop by the police,*** *he drove on.*
  (Although he was asked to stop by the police, he drove on.)
  Obwohl er von der Polizei aufgefordert wurde, …

- *Everyone should have access to a garden,* ***whether living*** *in the city or the countryside.*
  (Everyone should have access to a garden, whether they live in the city or the countryside.)
  …, egal, ob er oder sie in der Stadt oder auf dem Land lebt.

- ***If posted before 12 o'clock,*** *the letter should arrive tomorrow.*
  (The letter should arrive tomorrow if it is posted before 12 o'clock.)
  Wenn der Brief vor 12 Uhr eingeworfen wird, …

1 Skimming and scanning ➜ *SB (p. 179)*

SKIMMING

Step 1: Sieh dir die folgenden Textteile an, um zu sehen, worum es im Text geht:
- Überschrift und Unterüberschriften
- Bilder und Bildunterschriften
- den ersten Satz jedes Absatzes – dieser Satz ist meist der *topic sentence*, der die Hauptidee des Absatzes nennt
- den letzten Absatz, der oft eine Zusammenfassung des Textes enthält.

Step 2: Fasse für dich selbst den Text in ein paar Worten zusammen. Wenn dir das ohne Probleme gelingt, dann weißt du, um was es in dem Text geht – und dass dein Skimming erfolgreich war.

TIPP: Mache dir um unbekannten Wortschatz erst mal keine Gedanken – dafür ist Zeit, wenn du feststellst, dass der Text für dich geeignet ist.

SCANNING

Step 1: Überlege dir *keywords,* die für dein Thema oder deine Frage relevant sind. Suchst du z. B. nach den Öffnungszeiten eines Museums, dann könnten das Wörter sein wie *open, hours* oder *days.*

Step 2: Überfliege den Text und suche nach den *keywords.* Du kannst dabei mit dem Finger in einer „S-Form" durch den Text gehen.

Step 3: Lies die Textstelle, die dein *keyword* enthält, um zu sehen, ob sie die gewünschten Informationen enthält. Wenn nicht, scanne weiter.

TIPP: Wenn du mit Texten im Internet arbeitest, kann dein Browser dir viel Arbeit abnehmen. Mit Strg+F (Cmd+F am Mac) kannst du nach deinen *keywords* suchen und nur die Textstellen lesen, in denen ein *keyword* markiert ist.

2 Marking up a text ➜ *SB (p. 179)*

Step 1: Lies die Aufgabe genau und überlege, welche Informationen du zur Beantwortung brauchst. Behalte dies beim Lesen des Textes im Kopf.

Step 2: Markiere nur Informationen (z. B. durch Unterstreichen oder Einkreisen oder mit einem Textmarker). Oft reicht es, ein oder zwei Wörter in einem Satz zu markieren.

Step 3: Mach dir Notizen am Rand, z. B. kurze Überschriften oder Stichwörter, die den Inhalt zusammenfassen. (➜ *SMC 36*)

TIPP:
1. Verwende unterschiedliche Farben für unterschiedliche Aufgaben/Fragestellungen.
2. Markiere wirklich nur Stichwörter, sonst wird es unübersichtlich.

3 The stages of writing ➜ *SB (p. 180)*

Du solltest deine Texte stets gut planen und zuerst einen Entwurf erstellen, den du dann überarbeitest, bis das Ergebnis so ist, wie du es haben willst – leicht zu verstehen und ohne Fehler. Dieses Vorgehen braucht Zeit, aber es macht deine Texte besser.

PLANUNGSPHASE

Step 1: Plane dafür ausreichend Zeit ein. Denke über folgende Fragen nach:
- Über welches Thema willst du schreiben?
- Was genau sollst du tun (beschreiben, erläutern, zusammenfassen ...)?
- Welche Dinge musst du für den geforderten Text beachten?

Step 2: Dann solltest du
- alle nötigen Informationen für dein Thema **recherchieren** (➜ *SMC 22*),
- Ideen/Argumente sammeln und sortieren
- eine **Outline** für deinen Text (z. B. einen Bericht) schreiben. (➜ *SMC 7*)

TIPP: Wenn du mehr Informationen zum Verfassen guter Texte haben möchtest, sieh dir auch die folgenden Skills files an:
- **SMC 22:** Internet research
- **SMC 4:** Structuring texts
- **SMC 5:** Writing good sentences
- **SMC 6:** Writing a formal letter or email
- **SMC 7:** Making an outline
- **SMC 8:** Argumentative writing
- **SMC 9:** Writing a summary
- **SMC 10:** Revising texts
- **SMC 11:** Revising and improving electronic texts

ENTWURFSPHASE

Jetzt schreibe deinen ersten Entwurf:
- Füge deiner Outline **linking words** (➜ *SMC 5*) und **topic sentences** hinzu (➜ *SMC 4*).
- Beginne für jede neue Idee einen neuen Absatz.
- Führe deine Ideen aus und gib Beispiele (wenn das die Textsorte erfordert).
- Überlege, wie dein Text enden soll. Wenn du das weißt, ist es leichter, eine gute hinführende Einleitung zu schreiben. (➜ *SMC 4*)

ÜBERARBEITUNGSPHASE
- Liest sich der Text gut? Ist er logisch aufgebaut und hat er eine **gute Struktur**? (➜ *SMC 4*)
- Sieh dir die verschiedenen **sprachlichen Aspekte** deines Textes an: Grammatik, Rechtschreibung etc. (➜ *SMC 5, SMC 10, SMC 11*)
- Schreibe deinen Text noch einmal. Verbessere alles, was im Entwurf noch nicht gepasst hat. Wenn du **Feedback** bekommen hast, sieh es dir genau an und entscheide dann, was du davon für deinen Text übernehmen möchtest.

4 Structuring texts ➜ SB (p. 181)

SB (p. 181)

STRUCTURE

Ein guter Text besteht in der Regel aus den folgenden drei Teilen:

- **Einleitung *(introduction)***: Hier steht, worum es in dem gesamten Text geht. An dieser Stelle kann auch ein Problem genannt werden, das in dem Text erörtert werden soll.
- **Hauptteil *(main body)***: Dieser Teil ist in mehrere Absätze gegliedert und präsentiert die Details (Fakten, Beispiele etc.) zu deinem Thema.
- **Schluss *(conclusion)***: Hier gibst du deinem Text ein passendes, interessantes Ende.

PARAGRAPHS

Längere Texte sind einfacher zu lesen und schneller zu verstehen, wenn sie in Absätze eingeteilt sind. Dabei solltest du folgende Dinge beachten:

- Fange für jeden neuen Aspekt einen neuen Absatz an.
- Beginne mit einem interessanten *topic sentence*.
- Beende deinen Text im letzten Absatz mit einer Zusammenfassung oder etwas Persönlichem.

TOPIC SENTENCES

Jeder Absatz sollte mit einem Einleitungssatz beginnen.

Dieser **topic sentence** beschreibt, worum es in dem Absatz geht. Wichtige Dinge, die du in einem *topic sentence* ansprechen kannst, sind z. B.

- **Orte:** *My trip to Berlin was exciting.*
- **Personen:** *The Beatles are one of the most famous bands in the world.*
- **Aktivitäten:** *Lots of people ride their bike every day.*

My Trip to New Orleans

Last summer I wanted to go to New Orleans because I like big cities.

First I had to find some information on New Orleans. So I went online and looked for websites about things to do in New Orleans. I found a website with some interesting information on the sights and I also found a list of hostels for New Orleans.

At home I started to plan for my trip. I read all the websites and took notes on museums, the sights and the best cheap cafes in the city. After a few days I knew where I wanted to go and what I wanted to do there.

I did not want to go to New Orleans alone, so I had to find someone to go with me. I called most of my friends and told them about my plan. Some of them did not want to spend their holidays in a big city and others had no money for the trip. But my friend Judith agreed to go with me. We decided to go in August.

Judith and I spent two lovely weeks in New Orleans. We went to the French Market and enjoyed the fantastic food there. We stayed in a lovely hostel and met lots of really nice people. Before we went home we spent a whole afternoon in the French Quarter.

This was one of the best summer holidays I ever had. Go to New Orleans – it's fantastic!

5 Writing good sentences ➜ SB (p. 182)

Gute Texte bestehen aus abwechslungsreichen Sätzen. Die folgenden Techniken helfen dir, den Stil deiner Texte zu verbessern.

Adjektive

Beschreibe Dinge, Orte und Menschen näher mit Adjektiven:

- *a **bright** face*
- *a **fantastic** trip*

Stell aber sicher, dass du **good, bad** und **nice** nicht zu häufig verwendest. Ersetze sie durch genauere Adjektive:

- *a **nice** teacher: a **friendly** teacher, a **helpful** teacher, …*
- *a **good** book: an **interesting** book, a **funny** book, …*

Adverbien

Verwende Adverbien, um Handlungen näher zu beschreiben, und Ausdrücke wie **really, very, a bit** etc., um Aussagen zu verdeutlichen oder zu verstärken:

- *They walked home **slowly**.*
- *She talked **quietly**.*
- *It was a **really** sad story.*
- *The houses are **very** high.*

Konjunktionen

Konjunktionen wie **and, but** oder **because** geben deinen Sätzen eine klare, gut nachvollziehbare Struktur:

- *We went to the London Eye, **but** it was very expensive.*

Relativsätze

Relativsätze verbinden Sätze oder geben mehr Informationen zu einer Sache oder einer Person:

- *This is the shop **which** sells the best ice cream in Berlin.*

Zeitangaben

Adverbiale Bestimmungen der Zeit helfen Lesenden, sich in Texten zeitlich zurechtzufinden. Verwende *time markers*, um …

- die **Reihenfolge von Ereignissen** zu verdeutlichen: *at first, next, finally, …*
- zu zeigen, **wie viel Zeit** zwischen einzelnen Ereignissen vergeht: *for half an hour, just two minutes later, …*
- zu verdeutlichen, **wie langsam oder schnell** etwas passiert: *immediately, it took hours, faster than I could look, …*
- zu sagen, wenn etwas **zeitgleich** passiert: *while I was waiting, during the lesson, as we came round the corner, …*
- die **Ereignisse eines Textes/einer Geschichte** zeitlich einzuordnen: *two summers ago, last Halloween, on my way home from school yesterday, …*

6 Writing a formal letter or email ➔ SB (p. 183)

Wenn du einen Brief oder eine Mail an eine Organisation, einen potenziellen Arbeitgeber oder Ähnliches schreibst, sollte dein Schreiben gewissen formalen Regeln folgen.
Schreibe **deine Adresse** (ohne Namen) oben rechts. Verwende keine typisch deutschen Buchstaben wie ä, ö, ü oder ß.

Schreibe die volle Anschrift (mit Namen, wenn du ihn weißt) des **Adressaten** auf die linke Seite.

Schreibe das **Datum** auf die rechte Seite.

Sage kurz im **Betreff**, worum es geht.

Beginne deinen Brief/deine Mail mit *Dear Sir or Madam,* wenn du keinen genauen Ansprechpartner hast. Ansonsten schreibe *Dear Mr/Mrs/Ms …* (mit Komma danach, in den USA auch oft mit Doppelpunkt). Fange danach immer groß an.

Nenne den **Grund des Schreibens** im ersten Absatz.
- Ergänze weitere Informationen in den folgenden Absätzen.
- Verwende **Langformen** *(I am/We are/I would)* **statt Kurzformen** *(I'm/We're/I'd)* und Abkürzungen.

Wenn du den Adressaten um etwas bittest (z. B. Informationen), **bedanke dich** im Voraus.

Beende das Schreiben mit *Yours sincerely,* wenn du den Namen des Ansprechpartners kennst; ansonsten schreibe *Yours faithfully.* (Tippe deinen Namen am Ende des Briefs, aber lass ausreichend Platz für deine **Unterschrift.**

Kruemelstrasse 12
12345 Berlin
Germany

John Keats
Donne House
Ipswich IP3 4BA
United Kingdom

3 March 2019

Enquiry about exchange programme

Dear Mr Keats,

I am writing to enquire about the exchange programme which I saw advertised in The English Magazine.

I have been studying English at school for six years now and I would like to take part in an exchange programme to improve my English.

Could you please tell me if you offer any exchange programmes for one month in the summer? It would be helpful to know about dates, application procedures and the cost of such an exchange. Any additional information would be very welcome.

Thank you for your help. I look forward to hearing from you soon.

Yours sincerely,

Paul Panther

Paul Panther

7 Making an outline ➔ SB (p. 184)

Jede Art von Text profitiert davon, wenn du dir vorab überlegst, was du in welcher Reihenfolge schreiben willst. Damit leistest du schon eine Menge Vorarbeit und erleichterst dir das Schreiben.

- Für eine Erörterung (➔ *SMC 8*) kannst du in deiner Outline die Argumente sortieren, die du im Text bringen möchtest.
- Bei einer Zusammenfassung (➔ *SMC 9*) kannst du hier die wichtigsten Punkte festhalten.

Outline
1. *Title*
2. *Introduction*
   Keywords
3. *Main body*
   Sub-heading
   Keywords
4. *Conclusion*
   Keywords

8 Argumentative writing ➔ SB (p. 184)

Wenn du eine Erörterung schreibst – also schriftlich für oder gegen etwas argumentierst –, solltest du deinen Text gut strukturieren und und schlüssig präsentieren.

PLANUNGSPHASE

Step 1: Lies die Aufgabe sorgfältig durch.
Step 2: Sammle Ideen und mache erste Notizen. Schreibe alle Argumente pro und contra auf, die dir einfallen.
Step 3: Ordne deine Argumente, z. B. in Form einer Outline (➔ *SMC 7*). Hebe das wichtigste Argument hervor – damit solltest du deinen Hauptteil beenden, denn das merken sich die Lesenden am ehesten.

SCHREIBPHASE

Step 1: Schreibe deine Einleitung. Sage kurz, um welches Thema es geht, ohne deine eigene Meinung dazu zu äußern.
Step 2: Im Hauptteil präsentierst du dann die Argumente, die du dir überlegt hast.

Outline/Notes
1. *Introduction*
   Introduce the topic
2. *Main body*
   1st paragraph: arguments con
   – argument 1
   – argument 2 etc.
   2nd/3rd paragraph: arguments pro
   – argument 1
   – argument 2 etc.
   End with strongest argument!
3. *Conclusion*
   Sum up your arguments.
   Give your opinion.

9 Writing a summary ➔ SB (p. 185)

PLANUNGSPHASE

Step 1: Lies den Text genau. Mach dir Notizen (➔ *SMC 36*) oder markiere wichtige Stellen im Text (➔ *SMC 2*).

Step 2: Beantworte die *wh*-Fragen **Who? What? Where? When? Why?** zum Text. Du kannst dir Stichwörter am Rand machen.

Who? *Who does something? Who is the text about?*
What? *What happens? What does person X do?*
Where? *Where does it take place?*
When? *When does it take place?*
Why? *Why does person X act this way? Why does something happen?*

Step 3: Entscheide, welche Textteile wichtige Informationen enthalten. Beispiele, Vergleiche, direkte Rede oder Zahlen und Ähnliches gehören nicht in eine Zusammenfassung.

LANGUAGE HELP: Folgende *phrases* können dir bei der Einleitung helfen:
- *The story/text is about …*
- *The text deals with …*
- *The article/text shows …*

SCHREIBPHASE

Step 1: Schreib einen ersten Entwurf deiner Zusammenfassung:
- Beginne mit einer Einleitung, in der wichtige Informationen wie Titel, Autor/in, Thema und Hauptaussage des Textes stehen. Wenn du einen Zeitungsartikel zusammenfasst, solltest du hier auch die Quelle nennen.
- Verwende immer das **simple present**. Ausnahme hiervon: Wenn der Autor etwas beschreibt, das in der Vergangenheit oder der Zukunft liegt, z. B. in einem Zeitungsartikel, kannst du das auch so wiedergeben. Beispiel: *The writer **describes** the festival in New York, which **started** on Saturday, 4th April.*
- Kopiere den Text nicht, sondern benutze deine eigenen Worte.

Step 2: Überarbeite deine Zusammenfassung:
- Hast du alle wichtigen Aspekte genannt?
- Hast du unwichtige Details weggelassen?
- Ist dein Text durchgängig im *simple present* (außer in den genannten Ausnahmen)?
- Hast du deine Textteile gut verbunden? Ist dein Text logisch aufgebaut und gut zu verstehen?
- Vergiss auch nicht, den Text auf Rechtschreibung und Zeichensetzung zu checken. (➔ *SMC 10, SMC 11*)

10 Revising texts ➔ SB (p. 186)

TEXTÜBERARBEITUNG

1 **Stimmt die Struktur?**
Jeder Text braucht
- eine Einleitung, die in das Thema einführt,
- einen Hauptteil, der das Thema ausführt,
- einen Schluss, der alles auf den Punkt bringt. (➔ *SMC 4*)

2 **Stimmt der Aufbau der Absätze?**
Jeder Absatz
- befasst sich mit einem zusammenhängenden Gedanken,
- beginnt mit einem ***topic sentence***, der diesen Gedanken einführt. (➔ *SMC 4*)

3 **Stimmen die Verknüpfungen?**
Gute *linking words*
- schaffen Verbindungen zwischen Sätzen oder Satzteilen,
- helfen, Zusammenhänge verständlich zu machen. (➔ *SMC 5*)

4 **Sind die Zeitangaben richtig gesetzt?**
Time markers
- helfen, sich z. B. in einer Geschichte zurechtzufinden,
- machen das Geschehen anschaulicher. (➔ *SMC 6*)

5 **Enthält der Text Adjektive und Adverbien?**
Adjektive und Adverbien
- erlauben nähere Beschreibungen von Personen und Dingen,
- machen Texte anschaulicher. (➔ *SMC 5*)

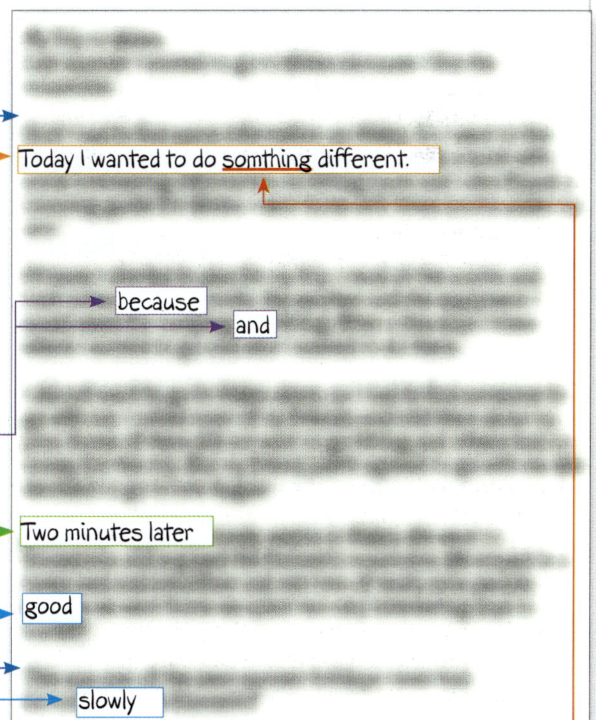

6 **Hat der Text sprachliche/grammatikalische Fehler?**
Überprüfe deinen Text
- auf Rechtschreibung und Satzzeichen,
- auf grammatische Formen, z. B. Verbformen, Satzbau (*word order*) usw.

11 Revising and improving electronic texts ➜ SB (p. 187)

KORREKTUR

- Nutze die Überprüfungsfunktion deines Textverarbeitungsprogramms. Sieh dir aber alle gemeldeten Fehler genau an, denn nicht alles ist auch wirklich falsch.
- Lies deinen Text trotzdem noch einmal Korrektur, weil nicht alle Fehler erkannt werden (z. B. wenn ein Tippfehler zu einem anderen korrekten Wort führt, das aber im Kontext nicht passt, wie *the* ***win*** *in the trees* statt *the* ***wind*** *in the trees*).

LAYOUT

- Lass genügend Abstand an den **Rändern** (meist reichen die voreingestellten Ränder, also 2,5 cm).
- Richte den Text **linksbündig** aus, denn das ist am besten lesbar. (Ausnahme: Die Überschrift kann zentriert sein, ebenso wie ein Zitat zum Einstieg.)
- Zwischenüberschriften lockern den Text auf und machen das Lesen leichter.
- Überlege dir gut, wo du Bilder einbaust: Bilder, die einen Inhalt im Text veranschaulichen, sollten auch möglichst nah an dieser Textstelle platziert werden.

TIPP: Wichtig: Denk dran, vor der Überprüfung deines Textes die Rechtschreibüberprüfung auf „Englisch (Großbritannien)" einzustellen.

TIPP: Wenn dein Text der Öffentlichkeit zugänglich gemacht wird, z. B. auf der Schulwebseite, musst du vor der Verwendung von Bildern die Urheber um Erlaubnis fragen. (➜ *SMC 22, 23, 24*)

12 Mediating written or spoken information ➜ SB (p. 188)

Wenn du Informationen in einer anderen Sprache wiedergeben sollst, geht es nicht darum, alles zu übersetzen, sondern es kommt darauf an, die wichtigsten Informationen herauszusuchen.

Schriftliche Informationen

- Scanne den Text gezielt nach den geforderten Informationen. (➜ *SMC 1*)
- Mach dir keine Sorgen, wenn du nicht jedes Wort verstehst. Das ist oft nicht nötig, um die wichtigen Punkte zu erfassen.
- Wenn der Text länger ist und du viele Informationen im Blick behalten musst, markiere die wichtigsten Textstellen. (➜ *SMC 2*)
- Mach dir Notizen in deinen eigenen Worten. (➜ *SMC 36*)

Mündliche Informationen

- Achte beim Hören gezielt auf die gesuchten Informationen. (➜ *SMC 21*)
- Mach dir Notizen (➜ *SMC 36*)
- Überlege, wie du deine Notizen am besten in der anderen Sprache wiedergeben kannst.

TIPP: Bei Mediation im Unterricht hast du in der Regel eine Aufgabenstellung, die dir sagt, worauf du beim Lesen oder Hören achten musst bzw. welche Stellen du wiedergeben sollst. Konzentriere dich beim Lesen auf diese Stellen *(scanning)* bzw. mach dir gezielt Notizen.

TIPP: Wenn du den Inhalt eines Textes schriftlich in einer anderen Sprache wiedergeben sollst, achte darauf, dass deine Mediation nicht länger ist als ca. 35–40% des Originaltextes. (➜ *SMC 9*)

13 Selecting relevant information ➜ SB (p. 188)

Manchmal gibt es keine gezielten Fragen oder Aufgabenstellungen dazu, welche Informationen du aus einem Text heraussuchen sollst. In der Regel hast du aber trotzdem Anhaltspunkte, die sich aus der Situation ergeben oder aus dem, was dir dein Gegenüber erzählt hat.

Wenn du in einer solchen Situation bist, helfen folgende Hinweise:

- Analysiere die Situation, um abzuschätzen, um welche Informationen es gehen könnte (Restaurant, Bahnhof, Flughafen usw.).
- Wenn du unsicher bist, frage nach.
- Übersetze wichtige Stichworte direkt, wenn du die Wörter kennst.
- Umschreibe Begriffe, die du nicht kennst.

TIPP: Wenn du Informationen wiedergibst, kannst du oft Details zu einem Begriff zusammenfassen. Wenn z. B. in einem Text *Twitter, Facebook, tumblr* und *Pinterest* vorkommen, kannst du *social media* sagen, anstatt alle aufzuzählen.

14 Paraphrasing ➜ SB (p. 189)

Es fällt dir eventuell manchmal schwer, mündliche Aussagen oder Texte auf Englisch wiederzugeben, z. B. weil dein Wortschatz nicht ausreicht, dir bekannte Wörter „im Stress" der Situation nicht einfallen oder spezielle Fachbegriffe auftauchen.

Wenn dir das passiert, dann solltest du versuchen, diese Wörter zu umschreiben, z. B. mithilfe von Relativsätzen wie:

It's somebody/a person who …   *It's something that you use to …*
It's an animal that …   *It's a place that/where …*

TIPP: Oft helfen beim Umschreiben auch **Synonyme** (gleiche Bedeutung) oder **Antonyme** (gegenteilige Bedeutung). Wenn du die weißt, kannst du z. B. sagen:

- *It's the same as …*
- *It's the opposite of …*

15 Cultural differences ➔ *SB (p. 189)*

Wenn du anderen Menschen hilfst, Texte oder Gehörtes zu verstehen, kann es neben Wortschatzproblemen auch noch andere Schwierigkeiten geben. Diese sind häufig in **kulturellen Unterschieden** begründet.

Dinge, die häufig zu **Missverständnissen** führen, sind z. B.
- **Temperaturen:** 30 Grad bei uns sind heiß, aber in den USA eher kalt, weil dort Temperaturen in Fahrenheit angegeben werden.
- **Längenangaben/Geschwindigkeit:** Bei uns wird das metrische System verwendet (Meter, Kilometer usw.), in den USA das *imperial system* mit *inch, yard* und *mile.* 75 mph (Meilen pro Stunde) sind z. B. ca. 120 km/h.

Wenn du feststellst, dass es zu einem Missverständnis gekommen ist, kannst du folgende Dinge probieren:
- Frage höflich nach, wo das Missverständnis liegt und versuche, es durch eine neue Erklärung zu beseitigen.
- Ergänze deine Erläuterung evtl. mit **Hintergrundinformationen:** Es kann sein, dass du bestimmte Dinge, die für dich völlig normal sind, erklären musst (z. B. Mülltrennung oder das Benutzen des Nahverkehrs).
- Sei offen für die Erklärungen, die du im Gegenzug bekommst – hierbei kannst du Dinge über das Land deines Gegenübers lernen.

16 Communicating in everyday situations ➔ *SB (p. 190)*

Es ist nicht immer einfach, sich mit Menschen aus anderen Ländern zu unterhalten. Neben der Sprachbarriere gibt es oft kulturelle Unterschiede. Die folgenden Schritte helfen dir, wenn du dich flüssig unterhalten willst:

Step 1: Beginne freundlich, z. B. mit etwas, was euch verbindet (der Ort, die Situation usw.).

Step 2: Halte das Gespräch am Laufen:
- Zeige dein Interesse, indem du Fragen stellst.
- Vermeide einsilbige Antworten, um nicht desinteressiert oder unfreundlich zu wirken.
- Wenn du etwas nicht verstehst, frage nach.
- Wenn du etwas nicht sagen kannst, versuche es zu umschreiben oder bitte deinen Gesprächspartner um Hilfe.

Step 3: Beende das Gespräch so freundlich, wie du es angefangen hast:
- Bedanke dich, wenn du um Hilfe gebeten hast.
- Verabschiede dich freundlich.

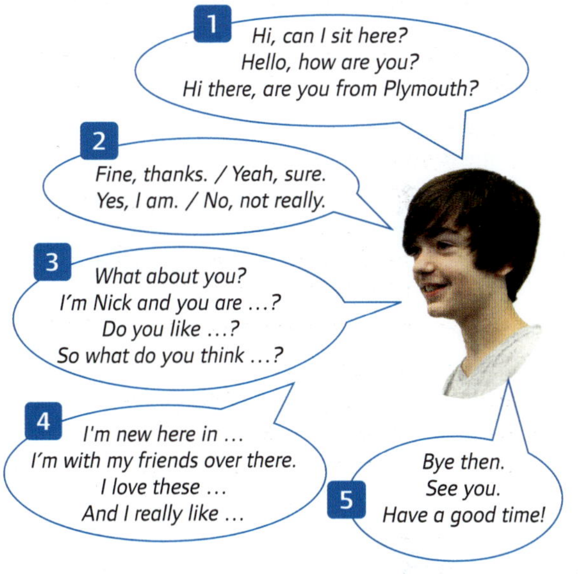

17 Having a discussion ➔ *SB (p. 191)*

In einer Diskussion tauscht man Meinungen und Ideen zu einem bestimmten Thema aus.

VORBEREITUNGSPHASE

Step 1: Bereite dich vor: Recherchiere Fakten und Beispiele. Überlege, was deine Meinung zu dem Thema ist. Mach dir Notizen.

Step 2: Halte deine Notizen für die Diskussion bereit, z. B. auf kleinen Zetteln.

Step 3: Überlege dir vorher ein Statement, das deine Meinung zum Thema gut ausdrückt.

DISKUSSION

Step 1: Starting the discussion: Sag deine Meinung (z. B. mithilfe der Eröffnung, die du dir überlegt hast).

Step 2: Continuing the discussion: Tausch deine Meinung mit anderen aus. Bleib höflich und sachlich. Hör den anderen zu und lass sie ausreden.
- Wenn du sprichst, bezieh dich auf die anderen und sag, weshalb du ihren Argumenten zustimmst (oder nicht).
- Stütz deine Meinung mit Fakten und Beispielen.

Step 3: Ending the discussion:
- Fass deinen Standpunkt noch einmal knapp zusammen.
- Versucht, Gemeinsamkeiten festzustellen, oder einigt euch darüber, dass es keine gemeinsame Lösung gibt *(agree to disagree).*
- Falls gefordert, einigt euch auf eine Lösung oder einen Kompromiss.

TIPP: Bei Rollenspielen musst du manchmal eine Meinung vertreten, die anders ist als deine eigene. Dann kannst du in deinen Notizen z. B. versuchen, Argumente und Gegenargumente einander gegenüberzustellen, um in der Diskussion schnell und gut reagieren zu können.

TIPP: Im Englischen ist man häufig weit weniger direkt als im Deutschen. Das bedeutet, dass du bei Diskussionen
- besonders gut zuhören musst, weil du sonst evtl. nicht genau mitbekommst, ob man dir zustimmt oder widersprichst;
- kurze, zu direkte Antworten wie *"No."* vermeiden solltest, weil sie unhöflich wirken.

18 Agreeing and disagreeing with people's opinions → SB (p. 191)

Es ist bei Diskussionen hilfreich, einige Redewendungen parat zu haben. Dann kannst du dich auf deine Argumente konzentrieren.

LANGUAGE HELP: Folgende Phrasen solltest du dir aufschreiben und lernen:

Stating your opinion	Agreeing	Disagreeing
In my opinion …	*I agree …*	*I'm afraid I don't quite agree …*
Well, I'd say …	*Exactly./Absolutely./…*	*I'm not sure about that.*
It's a fact that …	*You're quite right.*	*Do you really think so?*
Personally, I think…	*I think so too.*	*I'm not convinced that …*
If you ask me …	*You've got a good point there.*	*I doubt that (very much).*
I think/feel/believe …	*That's exactly how I see it.*	*I don't agree with you at all.*
First of all, I'd like to point out …	*That's true/right.*	*I disagree (completely).*
I'm certain that …	*I couldn't agree with you more.*	*It's not as simple as that.*

19 Taking part in an interview → SB (p. 192)

Bei Bewerbungsgesprächen helfen die folgenden 4 Ps:

PREPARE
- Finde so viel wie möglich über den Job und den Arbeitgeber heraus.
- Notiere mögliche Fragen, die du dem Arbeitgeber stellen kannst.
- Überleg dir aber auch, welche Fragen man dir stellen könnte, und bereite Antworten darauf vor.

PRACTISE
- Übe das Bewerbungsgespräch mit einem Partner/einer Partnerin.
- Gib deinem Partner/deiner Partnerin die Fragen, die du von deinem Arbeitgeber erwartest, und beantworte sie. Sag ihm/ihr auch, dass er/sie dir ruhig unerwartete Fragen stellen soll. So übst du, darauf zu antworten.

PRESENT
- Überleg dir, was du zu dem Bewerbungsgespräch anziehen möchtest. Die Auswahl der Kleidung hängt vom Arbeitgeber ab.
- Stell sicher, dass du pünktlich bist. Finde vorher heraus, wie du zum Ort des Gesprächs kommst. Plane Zeit für Unvorhergesehenes ein. Es ist immer besser, zehn Minuten zu früh als zu spät zu sein.

PARTICIPATE
- Stell dich am Anfang vor und lächle dabei freundlich.
- Lass dir Zeit, Fragen zu beantworten, besonders wenn es unerwartete Fragen sind. Antworte nicht mit *"Yes."* oder *"No."*, sondern versuche, Fragen ausführlich und höflich zu beantworten.
- Wenn du eine Frage nicht verstehst, frag nach.
- Verabschiede dich am Ende des Gesprächs mit einem freundlichen Lächeln und bedanke dich.

TIPP: Achte auch auf deine nonverbale Kommunikation – wie du stehst, gehst, sitzt – und sieh deinem Gegenüber in die Augen.

20 Viewing → SB (p. 193)

Es gibt viele Elemente, die die Atmosphäre und die Wirkung eines Films beeinflussen:
- Genre: Handelt es sich um einen Dokumentarfilm (documentary), einen Spielfilm (feature film) wie z. B. thriller, science-fiction/sci-fi movie, comedy oder ein drama? Oder ist es ein Videoclip oder ein Werbefilm?
- Story: Wo und wann spielt der Film (setting)? Besetzung der Rollen (cast), Schauplatz (location), Handlung (plot).
- Camera: Erst durch die Bilder der **Kamera** ist der Zuschauer in der Lage, einen Film wahrzunehmen. Die Kamera stellt das Blickfeld her und begrenzt es gleichzeitig, z. B. hinsichtlich der Beziehung der Charaktere zueinander. Auch die Stimmung oder Spannung in einer Szene wird von der Kameraführung beeinflusst. Dafür gibt es z. B. folgende Mittel:
  - Shots: Die **Kameraeinstellung** beeinflusst, wie man Szenen wahrnimmt, ob z. B. Personen oder Objekte als Nahaufnahme (close-up), aus der mittleren Distanz (medium shot) oder als Totale (long shot) gefilmt sind.
  - Editing: Filme werden in der Regel nicht chronologisch gedreht und auch nicht nur mit einer einzigen Kamera, d. h. am Ende der Dreharbeiten müssen viele einzelne Shots zusammengefügt werden. Dieser **Filmschnitt** bestimmt, wie eine Szene wirkt. Er bestimmt auch den Rhythmus – lange Einstellungen mit wenigen Schnitten wirken eher ruhig, können aber auch große Spannung erzeugen, während schnelle, harte Schnitte eher actiongeladen wirken.
- Soundtrack: Die **Musik**, die für eine Szene gewählt wird, hat großen Einfluss darauf, wie man die Szene wahrnimmt. Eine Actionszene wird meist mit schneller, lauter Musik unterlegt, eine romantische Szene eher mit ruhiger, leiser Musik. Dies verstärkt die Wirkung des Gesehenen.

21 Listening strategies ➜ *SB (pp. 194–195)*

LISTENING FOR DETAIL

- Überleg dir vorher, auf welche Informationen du achten musst.
  - Bei einem Wetterbericht sind das z. B. Beschreibungen wie *sunny, cloudy, chance of rain* etc., bei Bahnhofsansagen z. B. Wörter wie *platform* oder Orte und Zeiten.
  - Höre dann gezielt auf solche Wörter und notiere sie. (➜ *SMC 36*)
- Manchmal können dir Signalwörter helfen, dem Inhalt zu folgen:
  - Gründe, Folgen: *because, so, so that, …*
  - Vergleiche: *larger/older/… than, as … as, more, most, …*
  - Reihenfolge: *before, after, then, next, later, …*

TIPP: Im Unterricht kannst du Texte oft zweimal hören und hast weitere Hilfen:
- Sieh dir die Aufgabenstellung an: Was sollst du heraushören?
- Sieh dir Titel und Bilder an.
- Vergleiche nach dem Hören mit einem Partner/einer Partnerin, was ihr verstanden habt.
- Vervollständige deine Notizen sofort.

LISTENING FOR GIST

- Mach dir keine Sorgen, wenn du nicht jedes Wort verstehst – das brauchst du nicht, um dem Inhalt oberflächlich folgen zu können. Überlege dir anhand der Aufgabe, um was es gehen könnte, und konzentriere dich darauf.
- Versuch, von den Aussagen, die du verstehst, auf Inhalte zu schließen, die noch kommen könnten.

22 Internet research ➜ *SB (pp. 195–196)* MK

- Überleg, was die wichtigsten **Stichwörter** für dein Thema sind. Für das Thema „The Beatles in Hamburg" wären *Beatles* und *Hamburg* ein guter Start.
- Gib deine Stichwörter in eine **Suchmaschine** ein. Je mehr gute Stichwörter du eingibst, desto genauer sind die Ergebnisse. In der Infografik rechts kannst du sehen, wie du an ganz spezielle Informationen kommen kannst.
- Verwende möglichst Suchmaschinen, die deine Suchen nicht tracken, um deine Privatsphäre zu schützen.
- Sieh dir mehrere **Suchergebnisse** an, um zu prüfen, ob sie passen. Wenn du schnell ein bestimmtes Wort wie *Hamburg* finden willst, dann kannst du mit der Tastenkombination *Strg + F* (Mac: Cmd + F) danach suchen. Das Wort wird dann auf der Seite markiert und du kannst schnell sehen, ob die Information relevant ist.
- Achte darauf, wer die Webseite erstellt hat, um die **Qualität** der Suchergebnisse einzuschätzen. Sind sie wohl zuverlässig (Online-Lexikon, bekannte Medien) oder eher persönliche Meinungen (Forum, Fan-Seite …)?
- Kopiere nicht einfach ganze Artikel aus dem Internet. Mach dir Notizen und verwende deine eigenen Worte, um die Inhalte wiederzugeben.
- Setz dir ein Zeitlimit für deine Recherche und ordne dann dein Material. Prüfe, ob dir etwas fehlt, und such ggf. gezielt nur noch nach diesen Informationen.
- Leg alle interessanten Materialien zu deinem Thema in einem eigenen Ordner ab. Dann kannst du sie dir später genauer ansehen und auswählen, was du nutzen möchtest.

Internet research
Tipps und Tricks

Wenn du ganz spezifische Informationen suchst, helfen diese Tricks:

Was du suchst: Artikel aus der *Wikipedia*, in denen du Informationen über die Zeit der Beatles in Hamburg findest.
Wie du danach suchst:
site: wikipidia.com "the beatles" "hamburg"

site:	**" "**
sucht nur auf der genannten Seite	sucht die exakten Begriffe und erzwingt das Vorkommen im Suchergebnis

Was du suchst: Einen englischsprachigen Bericht, am liebsten als PDF, über den Lebensraum von Füchsen.
Wie du danach suchst:
filetype:pdf intitle:habitat of *fox

filetype:	**intitle:**	*****
sucht nur diesen Dateityp (pdf, doc, jpg usw.)	zeigt nur Ergebnisse, in denen dieses Wort im Titel auftaucht	sucht auch Worte wie Red Fox, Black Fox, Desert Fox usw.

TIPP: Du kannst bei einfachen Suchanfragen auch direkt die Frage ins Suchfeld eingeben, z. B. *What is 20 oz in grams?* Die Suchmaschine sucht sich dann selbst die relevanten Stichworte heraus – hier *20 oz* und *grams* – und liefert die Antwort. Bei komplexeren Suchanfragen sind die Antworten oft besser, je genauere Suchbegriffe du dir überlegst.

23 Creating a good layout for a page or poster ➜ *SB (p. 197)* MK

- Sortiere die **Informationen**, die du vermitteln willst: Was ist wichtig? Was ist ein Unterpunkt? Hast du Beispiele für Thesen/Argumente?
- Gib deinem Produkt eine klare **Struktur**: Texte haben meist drei Teile (Einleitung, Hauptteil, Schluss), während Poster häufig aus Aufzählungen wichtiger Punkte bestehen.
- Beginne für jeden neuen Gedanken einen neuen Absatz bzw. einen neuen Stichpunkt.
- Eine **Überschrift** verdeutlicht, worum es in deinem Text geht. Wenn es in deinem Produkt um mehrere Themen geht, dann kannst du für einzelne Abschnitte auch **Zwischenüberschriften** verwenden. Das gibt dem Ganzen eine klare Struktur und hilft den Lesenden, sich schnell zu orientieren.
- Ergänze dein Produkt mit **passenden Fotos, Videos, Audios, Statistiken** etc. Vergiss nicht anzugeben, woher die Medien stammen (➜ *SMC 22, SMC 24*)
- Wenn nicht auf den ersten Blick erkennbar ist, was ein Bild zeigt, füge **Bildunterschriften** ein.
- Formatiere dein Produkt so, dass es gut lesbar ist. Dabei ist das Medium wichtig – für einen ausgedruckten Handzettel kannst du andere **Schriftarten** wählen als für einen Text, der am Bildschirm gelesen wird. (➜ *SMC 23*) Für ein Poster (z. B. für einen *gallery walk*) muss die **Schriftgröße** größer sein als für einen Ausdruck. Eine große Schrift hilft dir auch, nicht zu viele Punkte auf dem Poster unterzubringen – hier ist weniger mehr.

24 Making good slides for an electronic presentation ➜ *SB (pp. 197–198)*

TEXT
- Verwende möglichst wenige Folien.
- Nutze **Aufzählungen** mit *keywords*, keine ganzen Sätze, und schreibe nicht mehr als sechs Zeilen auf eine Folie.
- Wähle eine ausreichende **Schriftgröße** (mindestens 30 pt, gerne mehr) und eine gut lesbare Schrift. Lass einen ausreichend großen **Abstand** zwischen den Zeilen.
- Richte den **Text linksbündig** aus, außer du verfolgst ein ganz besonderes Ziel damit (z. B. zentriert zum Herausheben eines Zitats), aber mische die Ausrichtung nicht auf einer Folie.

ABBILDUNGEN
- Manche Inhalte kannst du gut nur mit einem passenden Bild oder einer Grafik statt mit Worten ausdrücken.
- Suche ein Bild, dass die Aussage deines Vortrags verdeutlicht, z. B. ein Foto, das ein Problem gut darstellt. Manchmal eignet sich auch eine Grafik, z. B. ein Diagramm.
- Wichtig: Bei allen Bildern, die du verwendest, musst du die Quelle angeben, d. h. den Fotografen/die Fotografin, den Illustrator/die Illustratorin etc. sowie den Ort, wo du das Bild gefunden hast. (Eine Suchmaschine ist keine Quellenangabe!)

25 Giving a presentation ➜ *SB (p. 198)*

Vorbereitung
- Sammle Informationen zu deinem Thema.
- Wähle eine Form der Präsentation aus, die das Thema gut veranschaulicht (Poster, Folie, Tafel …).
- Mach dir Notizen, z. B. auf nummerierten Karteikarten oder in einer App.
- Bereite deine Medien vor (Poster, Folie, Tafelanschrieb …). Schreibe groß und für alle gut lesbar.
- Übe deine Präsentation zu Hause vor einem Spiegel oder vor einem kleinen Publikum (Eltern, Großeltern, Freunde).

Durchführung
- Warte, bis es ruhig ist. Schau die Zuhörer/innen an.
- Erkläre, worüber du sprechen wirst und wie deine Präsentation aufgebaut ist.
- Lies nicht von deinen Karten ab, sondern sprich möglichst frei.

Schluss
- Sag, dass du zum Ende kommst. Bedanke dich fürs Zuhören.
- Frag die Zuhörer/innen, ob sie Fragen haben.

26 Talking about statistics ➜ *SB (p. 199)*

Wenn du Statistiken analysieren und vorstellen sollst, gehst du am besten wie folgt vor:

Step 1: Identifiziere, welche Art von Diagramm du vor dir hast – **pie chart**, **bar chart**, **line graph** oder **Tabelle** – und sieh dir die Quelle an:
- Ist die Quelle verlässlich?
- Sind die Angaben/Zahlen im Diagramm aktuell?

Step 2: Beschreibe das Diagramm/die Tabelle:
- Worum geht es? Welche Informationen gibt das Diagramm?
  The bar chart/pie chart/line graph/table/ … shows the different …/ compares the size/number of …/is about …/contrasts … with …
- Zeigen die Daten eine Entwicklung oder werden verschiedene Zeitpunkte miteinander verglichen?
  It shows … in contrast to … *The chart gives us information about who/what/how many/…*
- Werden absolute Zahlen oder Prozentangaben verwendet?
  The chart/table shows us the number of/percentage of … *It shows which percentage of …*

Step 3: Ziehe deine Schlussfolgerungen aus dem Diagramm/der Tabelle:
My main conclusion is that … *The most important thing I've learned is that …*
One thing that I hadn't realized before is …

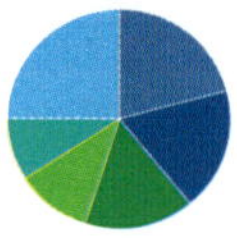
pie chart

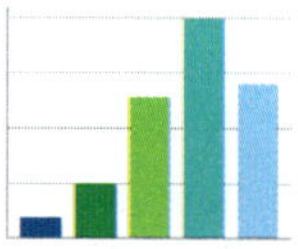
bar chart

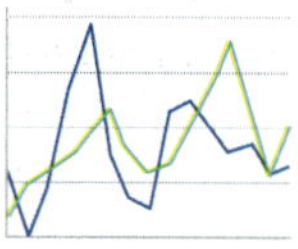
line graph

27 Describing and presenting pictures ➜ *SB (p. 200)*

1 Stell das Foto vor und sag, woher es kommt.
2 Beschreibe das Foto:
   – Sag, was wo zu sehen ist: *at the top/bottom* · *in the foreground/background* · *in the middle* · *on the left/right*
   – Diese Präpositionen sind auch hilfreich: *behind* · *between* · *in front of* · *next to* · *under* · *over*
   – Geh bei der Beschreibung in einer bestimmten Reihenfolge vor, z. B. von links nach rechts oder von oben nach unten.
3 Sag, was dir an dem Foto gefällt oder nicht.
4 Wenn du mit der Vorstellung des Fotos fertig bist, bedanke dich fürs Zuhören und erkundige dich, ob noch jemand Fragen hat.

28 Teamwork ➜ *SB (p. 200)*

Step 1: Legt Regeln für die Arbeit in der Gruppe fest, z. B. gegenseitig unterstützen, pünktlich arbeiten, einander zuhören usw.
Step 2: Sammelt Ideen für die Bearbeitung eures Themas. Wählt Unterthemen aus und legt die Arbeitsschritte fest.
Step 3: Verteilt Rollen und Aufgaben nach euren Interessen und Fähigkeiten. Wenn ihr euch nicht einigen könnt, hilft Auslosen oder Würfeln. Folgende Rollen solltet ihr auf jeden Fall verteilen: ***coordinator, writer*** und ***researcher***.
Step 4: Macht einen Zeitplan für eure Arbeiten, an den sich alle halten.
Step 5: Am Ende der Arbeit sollte ein Rückblick stehen: Besprecht, was gut war und wo ihr Verbesserungsmöglichkeiten seht.

29 Peer feedback ➜ *SB (p. 201)*

Bei deiner Rückmeldung solltest du drei Dinge beachten:
- Halte dich an die Punkte, zu denen du Rückmeldung geben sollst, z. B. die Aussprache und Verständlichkeit bei einem Dialog, die Rechtschreibfehler in einem Text, das Einhalten eines roten Fadens in einer Geschichte usw. Begründe deine Einschätzungen.
- Gib deine Rückmeldung mit Respekt – niemand soll sich angegriffen fühlen. Nenn zuerst Gelungenes und mach dann Verbesserungsvorschläge zu Punkten, die noch nicht so gelungen sind.
- Wenn du selbst eine Rückmeldung bekommst, überdenke die Vorschläge gut. Korrigiere die Fehler, die andere gefunden haben, und arbeite an den Stellen nach, wo du eventuell Probleme hattest.

30 Understanding new words ➜ *SB (p. 201)*

- Viele englische Wörter werden ähnlich wie im Deutschen geschrieben oder klingen ähnlich (z. B. *brochure, statue, insect*). Manche sehen auch einem Wort aus anderen Sprachen ähnlich, z. B. *voice (French: voix; Latin: vox)*.
- In manchen Wörtern stecken bekannte Teile, z. B. *bottle opener, snowshoe*.
- Präfixe und Suffixe wie *un-*, *re-* und *-er* helfen beim Erschließen: *listener* (*sb. who listens*), ***un**happy <> happy, **re**pay (pay back)*.
- Bilder zum Text zeigen oft Dinge, die du im Text vielleicht nicht verstehst.
- Der Kontext kann beim Verstehen helfen, z. B. *Let's hurry. The train **departs** in ten minutes.*

31 Using a dictionary ➜ *SB (p. 202)*

ZWEISPRACHIGE WÖRTERBÜCHER

Die Leitwörter *(running heads)* oben auf der Seite helfen dir, schnell zu finden, was du suchst. Auf der linken Seite steht das erste Stichwort, auf der rechten Seite das letzte Stichwort der Doppelseite.
- *resign* ist das **Stichwort** *(headword)*. Stichwörter sind alphabetisch geordnet: *r* vor *s*, *ra* vor *re*, *rhe* vor *rhi* usw.
- Die **kursiv gedruckten** Hinweise helfen dir, die für deinen Text passende Bedeutung zu finden.
- Die **Ziffern** 1, 2 usw. zeigen, dass ein Stichwort unterschiedliche Bedeutungen haben oder unterschiedlichen Wortarten angehören kann (z. B. Adjektiv, Nomen, Verb).
- **Beispielsätze und Redewendungen** sind dem Stichwort zugeordnet.
- **Unregelmäßige Verbformen**, besondere **Pluralformen**, die **Steigerungsformen der Adjektive** und ähnliche Hinweise stehen oft in Klammern oder sind kursiv gedruckt.
- Die **Lautschrift** gibt Auskunft darüber, wie das Wort ausgesprochen und betont wird.

resort

resign /rɪˈzaɪn/
1 BERUF • *als Vorsitzender usw* zurücktreten: ***He resigned from the company.*** Er verließ das Unternehmen.
2 (*job, post*) aufgeben (*Stelle, Posten*)
3 **resign oneself to something** sich mit etwas abfinden
resignation /ˌrezɪgˈneɪʃn/
1 BERUF • *bei Unternehmen* Kündigung; *von Minister usw* Rücktritt
2 **hand in one's resignation** *von Angestelltem* kündigen; *von Minister usw* sein Amt niederlegen
3 *Gemütszustand* Resignation
resigned /rɪˈzaɪnd/ (*look, sigh*) resigniert

EINSPRACHIGE WÖRTERBÜCHER

Wenn du selbst einen Text schreibst, kannst du ein einsprachiges Wörterbuch zu Hilfe nehmen. Hierin findest du mehr als in einem zweisprachigen Wörterbuch:
- Ein einsprachiges Wörterbuch erklärt die Bedeutung eines Worts auf Englisch. Da manche Wörter mehrere Bedeutungen haben, ist es wichtig, alle Einträge und Beispielsätze zu einem Wort zu lesen und mit deinem englischen Text zu vergleichen, um die korrekte Bedeutung herauszufinden.
- Das einsprachige Wörterbuch hilft dir, die passende Verbindung mit anderen Wörtern zu finden, z. B. mit Verben und Präpositionen oder in bestimmten feststehenden Wendungen. Das ist nützlich, wenn du nach den richtigen Wörtern für deinen englischen Text suchst.

deadly ['dedli] *adj*
1 *able or likely to kill people* {= lethal}: This is no longer a deadly disease.
deadly to The HSN virus is deadly to chickens.
a deadly weapon The new generation of biological weapons is more deadly than ever.
2 *(only before noun)* {= complete}:
a deadly secret Don't tell anyone – this is a deadly secret.
deadly serious *completely serious:* Don't laugh – I am deadly serious!
3 *(informal) very boring*: Many TV programmes are pretty deadly!

32 Using an online translator ➜ *SB (p. 203)*

Für **einzelne Wörter** kannst du *online translators* verwenden – sie funktionieren im Prinzip wie Wörterbücher. Das geht schnell, kann aber auch ein paar Nachteile haben:

- Ein Wörterbuch (online oder als Buch) gibt dir wesentlich mehr Informationen, u. a. Beispielsätze mit dem gesuchten Wort.
- Übersetzungsmaschinen geben dir oft nicht alle korrekten Übersetzungen, sondern nur ein oder zwei Möglichkeiten oder aber die gängigsten.
- Übersetzungsmaschinen bieten dir keinen Kontext, was es schwerer für dich macht, das richtige Wort zu finden.

Ganze Sätze oder gar Texte mit Übersetzungsmaschinen vom Deutschen ins Englische zu übertragen, ist keine gute Idee, weil die künstliche Intelligenz, die dahintersteckt, dabei immer noch zu viele Fehler macht. Vor allem bei folgenden Dingen haben Übersetzungsmaschinen Probleme:

- **Grammatik:** Da die Übersetzungsmaschinen von Wörtern ausgehen und nicht von der Satzstruktur, entstehen gerade bei komplexeren Sätzen schnell Fehler.
- **Idiome:** Aus demselben Grund sind auch Idiome und geflügelte Worte ein Problem, denn die Maschine kann die oftmals nicht-wörtliche Bedeutung nicht erkennen. Ein Beispiel: „Fällt dir die Decke auf den Kopf?“ kann völlig falsch mit *„Do you get the ceiling on your head?“* wiedergegeben werden.
- **Regionale Sprachbesonderheiten:** Manche Wörter und Ausdrücke sind regionalspezifisch (oder heute weniger gebräuchlich) und werden von *online translators* nicht erkannt, z. B. wenn „Feudel“ mit „Feudel“ statt mit *floor-cloth* übersetzt wird.

33 Using the Internet to improve your vocabulary ➜ *SB (p. 204)*

Das Internet bietet dir auch die Möglichkeit, dein Englisch zu verbessern und deinen Wortschatz zu erweitern.

LESEN UND SCHREIBEN

- Lies regelmäßig Blogs/Webseiten zu Themen, die dich interessieren.
- Lies Nachrichten online, z. B. auf den Seiten von Zeitungen wie dem *Guardian* (GB) oder der *New York Times* (USA).
- Lade dir kostenlose E-Books herunter. Das *Project Gutenberg* hat z. B. eine große Auswahl.
- Starte einen eigenen Blog und/oder kommentiere Artikel in anderen Blogs. Tausche dich so mit anderen Nutzern aus.

HÖREN UND SEHEN

- Finde Radiostationen online, z. B. *NPR, BBC World Service* oder *Voice of America,* oder suche Podcasts, die dich interessieren.
- Sieh dir regelmäßig Clips und Filme an. Seiten wie *YouTube* bieten jede Menge Nachrichtenclips oder auch Dokumentationen.
- Webseiten wie die des *British Council* oder der *BBC* bieten gute Podcasts zum Thema Englisch und Englischlernen.
- Auf Seiten wie *LibriVox* kannst du kostenlose Audiobücher herunterladen und anhören.

WORTSCHATZ

- Verwende Suchmaschinen als Ergänzung zum Rechtschreibcheck deines Schreibprogramms: Gib ein, was du geschrieben hast, und suche danach. Wenn du kaum Ergebnisse bekommst, solltest du deine Kollokation noch mal checken.
- Wenn du online nach Wörtern und Redemitteln suchst, ist eines der ersten Ergebnisse häufig ein Online-Wörterbuch, in dem du dann weitere Bedeutungen und häufige Kollokationen nachlesen kannst.
- Suchmaschinen versuchen, deine Suche vorherzusagen. Dies kannst du nutzen, um gängige Kollokationen und Wortkorrelationen zu finden. Beispiel: Du gibst *shower* ein und es werden auch *shower curtain, shower heads* und *shower thoughts* aufgelistet.

34 Ordering and structuring vocabulary ➜ *SB (p. 205)*

Einige der Formen, die du nutzen kannst, sind:

- Tabellen (***tables***)
- Diagramme (z. B. ***tree diagrams***)
- Mindmaps

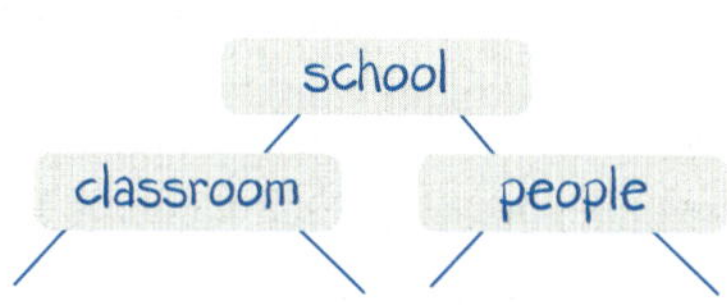

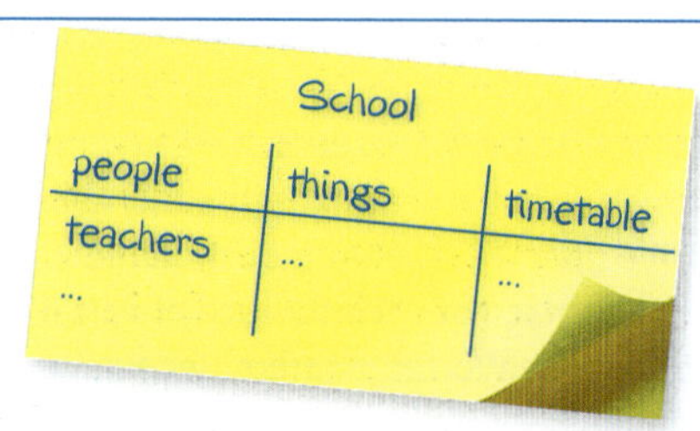

TIPP: Wenn du Wortschatz für einen Text zusammenstellst, solltest du daran denken, dass du nicht nur Nomen, sondern auch Verben, Adverbien, Adjektive etc. brauchst, sowie Varianten für Ausdrücke, die häufig vorkommen.

35 Working with a grammar ➜ SB (p. 206)

Die Grammatik lernst du im Schulbuch, aber es gibt natürlich auch eigenständige Grammatiken, die du zur Ergänzung nutzen kannst. Der Aufbau einer Grammatik ist dabei meist relativ ähnlich wie die Grammatik in diesem Buch.

Überschrift
Hier steht, worum es auf der Seite geht.

Zwischenüberschrift
Wenn ein Thema mehrere Unterthemen hat, gibt es meist entsprechende Unterüberschriften.

Erklärung/Regeln
Hier wird das Thema erklärt mit allem, was man dazu beachten muss. Oft gibt es hier auch noch einmal Unterteilungen.

Beispiele
Neben den Erläuterungen (oder darunter) sind Beispiele und Beispielsätze zu finden.

Zusammenfassung
Oft findet sich am Ende eines Themas oder Unterthemas noch einmal eine Zusammenfassung.

4.4 Das Verb *do* The verb *do*

4.4.1 Formen Forms

Das Verb *do* hat die Formen *do, does* (im ***simple present***) und *did* (im ***simple past***).
Die **infiniten Verbformen** (▸ 10.1) lauten:
- *do* (Infinitiv)
- *done* [dʌn] (Partizip Perfekt)
- *doing* (*ing*-Form)

Mit dem Partizip Perfekt *done* bildet man die **Perfektformen** *present perfect (have/has done), past perfect (had done)* und *future perfect (will have done)*.
Mit dem Infinitiv *do* bildet man die **Zukunftsformen** *(will do* und *am/is/are going to do)*.

simple present	*simple past*
I do	I did
you do	you did
he does [dʌz]	he did
she does	she did
it does	it did
we do	we did
you do	you did
they do	they did

4.4.2 Das Hilfsverb *do* The auxiliary verb *do*

a Man verwendet *do/does/did* zur Bildung von **Verneinungen, Fragen, Kurzantworten** und **Frageanhängseln** im *simple present* und *simple past*.

I don't go out very often.
What does this word mean?
Do you speak English? – Yes, I do.
Helen didn't forget your birthday, did she?

b Man verwendet *don't* (Langform: *do not*) zur **Verneinung des Imperativs**.

Don't go, please.
Do not touch.

c Man kann *do/does/did* verwenden, um das **Vollverb** zu **betonen**.
▸ Hervorhebung mit *do*: 1.6.1

I do ['du:] like the way she bakes her cakes.
Do hurry up.

4.4.3 Das Vollverb *do* The full verb *do*

a In der Bedeutung „machen", „tun", „verrichten", „erledigen" ist *do* ein Vollverb. Wie jedes **Tätigkeitsverb** kann es sowohl in der einfachen Form als auch in der Verlaufsform stehen.

Hurricanes do a lot of damage every year.
I'm still doing my homework.
Next week we're doing lots of activities.

b Verneinungen und **Fragen** im *simple present* und *simple past* bildet man ganz regelmäßig mit *do/does/did*.

We don't usually do much at the weekends.
Donald doesn't do much to help his parents.
Seth didn't do what his father wanted.
When did Jim do his exam?

Auf einen Blick
- Mit dem **Hilfsverb *do*** bildet man Verneinungen und Fragen: *I **don't** know. / **Do** you know?*
- Auch das **Vollverb *do*** braucht das **Hilfsverb *do***: *I **don't do** crosswords. / **Do** you **do** crosswords?*

Weitere Dinge
Je nach Grammatik und/oder Thema kann es z. B. auch noch nützliche Tipps oder Warnungen vor besonders häufigen Fehlerquellen geben.

36 Making and taking notes ➜ SB (p. 207)

Wenn du Informationen oder eigene Gedanken kurz für dich notierst, heißt das im Englischen **making notes**. Wenn du dir Notizen beim Lesen oder Zuhören machst, heißt das **taking notes**.
Für beide Varianten gelten aber die gleichen Grundsätze.

Step 1: Achte auf **keywords**, um deine Frage/Aufgabe zu beantworten oder den Inhalt eines Textes grob zu verstehen.
Step 2: Notiere nur die wichtigsten Informationen. Verwende **Abkürzungen und Symbole**, aber achte darauf, dass du immer dieselben verwendest, damit du deine Notizen später noch verstehst. Markiere offene Fragen.
Step 3: Geh im Anschluss an das Lesen oder Hören noch mal durch deine Notizen und ergänze evtl. fehlende Informationen.

TIPP: Wenn du kein eigenes System von Abkürzungen hast, kannst du z. B. auch diese verwenden:

the same as	=	*becomes/will be*	->	*important*	!	*open question*	??
not the same as	≠	*between*	b/w	*not*	x		
about the same as	≈	*in other words*	i.e.	*with*	w/		
and	+	*for example*	e.g.	*without*	w/o		

Checkpoint 1

1 WORDS Australia and the UK

vast/large, (mainly) rural, overcrowded, settled, convicts, Aboriginal/native/indigenous, exchanges, Aussies, flight/trip, easy-going, scenic/vast/wide/stunning, exotic/tropical, historical/old/lively/beautiful, mild, landmarks

2 AusE pronunciation

1 What time did your flight get in last night?
2 I bought a better pair of boots for when it gets wetter.
3 We can't see the trees very easily from here.
4 I must write a birthday card to my father this afternoon.

3 A Brit in Sydney

Being, visited, taking, forgetting, walking, filming, coming, believing, pulling, helping, cheering, clapping, turning, asked

4 What are they doing?

1 A 2 C

5 A conversation at the beach

a) B

b) 1 Singapore, London, Edinburgh 2 26 and a half hours 3 it will be colder there 4 can chat online, brother will visit 5 his dog (Rex) 6 in 1892 7 their accent is difficult to understand 8 they are/were police officers 9 go to school, do homework, help at home, be polite 10 16,950

Checkpoint 2

1 WORDS Learning to deal with money

chores, budget/work, value, run out of/spend, balance out, expenses, encourage/teach, piggy bank, account

2 Some tips on how to stay safe online

1 shouldn't, 2 should/ought to, 3 should/ought to, 4 shouldn't

3 Hadrian's Wall – history and attractions

b) 1 six years
2 You can start at Wallsend on the River Tyne and walk to Bowness-on-Solway on the Irish Sea. You can also do the tour in the other direction, i. e. start at Bowness-on-Solway.

4 The rise and fall of the British coal industry

a) 1 coal, Industrial Revolution: to produce steel, to power locomotives, steamships and machines in factories, to heat houses 2 coalfields in the Northeast: a lot of coal was mined there, 25 per cent of Britain's coal by 1913 3 new towns: appeared near the pits because miners' homes were built there 4 decline: cheaper to buy coal from abroad or use other sources of energy, steam railways replaced by diesel and electric trains, private households switched to central heating, increased awareness of environmental problems
5 situation improved: new jobs in modern industries
6 report from 2019: stated that mining towns and villages had not completely recovered, problems: unemployment, ill health, social disadvantage

b) fossil fuel – fossiler Brennstoff, sources of energy – Energiequellen, power – antreiben, heat – heizen, decline – Niedergang, replace – ersetzen, awareness – Bewusstsein, closures – Schließungen, recover – sich erholen, former – ehemalige(r, s) unemployment – Arbeitslosigkeit

Checkpoint 3

1 WORDS Describing character

a) 1 enthusiastic 2 ambitious/competitive 3 Hard-working 4 cautious 5 confident/self-confident 6 jealous

b) 1 irresponsible 2 dishonest 3 intolerant 4 impolite 5 impractical 6 unemotional 7 unreliable 8 irregular 9 disrespectful

2 Which tense?

1 was sent 2 have just been offered 3 were not/weren't asked 4 were given 5 have been shown 6 has been promised

3 How to write a letter of application

address, right, "Dear Sir or Madam", "Dr Mr/Mrs/Ms …", short, conclusion, "Yours sincerely"

Checkpoint 4

1 PRONUNCIATION Word stress

a) calendar democracy contribute agriculture rehearse complex visa poetic itinerary

2 What will they be doing?

1 'll be surfing 2 'll be taking 3 won't be living 4 will be playing

3 By the time you visit us …

1 'll/will have been 2 'll/will have passed 3 won't have finished 4 'll/will have arrived

4 An introduction to a presentation

Good morning everybody. I'm going to talk to you about Māori culture today. I've divided my talk into four parts. Firstly, I'll talk about the lives of the Māori when they were the only inhabitants of New Zealand. Secondly, I'll explain how Māori culture changed after the British had arrived. Thirdly, I'll present some facts about te reo, which is the Māori's language. I'll finish by talking about the positive developments for the indigenous people since the late 20th century. Let's start with the coming of the Māori to New Zealand.

5 Referring to pictures, posters and slides

1 show 2 look at 3 see 4 have 5 draw 6 compare, notice